WATER

For Thelma,

Wishing you God's
blessings now and always

Michael Ford

'At key moments, you may have to go through painful, disturbing experiences, just to grow up, to realize who you are and how life works ... They can take you, step by step, into your own undiscovered reality.' (Thomas Moore)

WATERSHED
Turning points on the spiritual road

MICHAEL FORD

DARTON·LONGMAN+TODD

For Kristine Pommert and David Coomes
and
Friends at Ripon College, Cuddesdon (2011–12)

Also to the memory of Guzler,
spiritual companion who observed the writing process day by day

First published in 2012 by
Darton, Longman and Todd Ltd
1 Spencer Court
140 – 142 Wandsworth High Street
London SW18 4JJ

© 2012 Michael Ford

The right of Michael Ford to be identified as the
Author of this work has been asserted in accordance with the
Copyright, Designs and Patents Act 1998.

ISBN: 978-0-232-52872-5

A catalogue record for this book is available from the British Library.

Printed and bound in Great Britain by Bell & Bain, Glasgow

CONTENTS

	Prelude	7
1	Choice and Cost	16
2	Searching and Becoming	30
3	Addiction and Grace	46
4	Stability and Change	60
5	Hurt and Healing	73
6	Loss and Hope	89
7	Illusion and Reality	99
8	Struggle and Faith	112
9	Abandonment and Trust	121
	Postlude	135
	Notes	139
	Acknowledgements	143

PRELUDE

A watershed is a ridge of high land dividing two areas drained by different river systems, a critical juncture which marks a change of course.

Few of us travel through life without, at some point, having to navigate our way through our own unchartered waters. These turning points are often a challenge to our basic humanity as much as to our spiritual development. They can send us spiralling downwards or they can be *kairos* moments, times for opportunity, growth and an unexpected change of direction.

Any spiritual journey is likely to involve an endless series of changes, struggles and turning points. It is a hard road to travel, according to the writer Wilkie Au, director of Spiritual Development Services in Los Angeles. The predictable crises of human life are outlined in the literature of developmental psychology which plots the pattern of adult growth as a zigzag of setbacks and frustrations. Unpredictable crises are events such as sudden illnesses, bereavements, career disappointments and interpersonal conflicts. 'Crises come unbidden into our lives; they are not chosen by us and they are not wanted by us.'

The Chinese word for 'crisis' involves two characters or ideograms – the first means danger, the second signifies opportunity. Au points out that, in the West, people tend to cast crises entirely in a negative light because of their inherent dangers. But the Chinese believe there is a positive dimension to a crisis in that it can also create an opportunity.

Au also speaks about 'annunciation moments in life'. Mary at the Annunciation is an inspiring model of both patience and courage during a time of crisis. In our own lives too, when we experience an inner stirring or a sense that something is shifting, we realise that we need to make a change of some sort without knowing where it might lead. This can rock the boat, not only for us but also for those close to us who have become accustomed to the status quo. Mary is a model of trust in God as we make that leap of faith.[1]

The perceptions we have of ourselves, the world around us or the place of faith in our lives can alter dramatically as our journeys move forward from the crossroads and sometimes follow surprising courses. These can prove to be lonely and fearful times as we readjust to the new landscape but we can also be led into a more profound understanding of ourselves and the spiritual quest.

This, then, is a book about facing those life-changing experiences that define the future. It is told largely through the stories of others which take us into many disparate worlds as women and men describe some of the turning points in their own lives and how they got through them. The encounters took place over many years and the conversations evolved into this book.

Time and again on my journalistic travels, I seem to have been drawn to people who have been faced with a watershed of one kind or another. Far from defeating them, however, the crisis has often precipitated interior growth. This was especially apparent when I arrived in New York City after the watershed of 9/11.

THE CRUCIBLE

It was dusk in Manhattan. The lamps irradiated the contours of his face. He was smiling but I could tell he had been through something. As I glanced again, the countenance was definitely that of joy and gratitude, yet there seemed also to be questions, almost etched in relief on his forehead. As I made my way through the throng, microphone in hand, the bulbs of the camera crews lit up the

PRELUDE

expression. In the elegant setting of a mid-town complex, the officer pulled a young woman close to his dark uniform and beamed for the photographers. He was made to feel like a veteran war hero but, as the daughter beside him knew only too well, he was actually being hailed a survivor.

On September 11, 2001, Lieutenant Colonel Thomas J. Cleary III had been at the Pentagon in Washington DC. He escaped death literally by inches as one of the hijacked planes crashed into the building, obliterating the room beside him and killing many of his colleagues. Six months on, he was being honoured as a hero as part of the St Patrick's Day celebrations in New York City. As the American Press teams moved on, I moved swiftly in, introducing myself to Lt Col. Cleary who shook me warmly by the hand, pulled over two chairs and started to tell me his story. As I listened intently, I was struck again by the privilege of being alongside others at critical times in their lives: asking, opening, listening, empathising.

Thomas Cleary, a devout Roman Catholic, told me that the army personnel department, for whom he was working, had recently moved into 'a new wedge' of the Pentagon that had been renovated for the first time in half a century. He had been sitting at his desk in what had been known as the C and D rings of the fourth corridor.

'When the first plane hit the World Trade Center, there was obviously a buzz in the office,' he said. 'My boss had CNN on and we naturally migrated to his office. We were all sitting there, watching the TV, when the second plane flew into the second tower, much to our complete amazement and apoplexy.

'After watching the drama unfold, we went back to our desks. I tried to call my wife. But I couldn't reach her so I called a friend who works 100 yards away. I was about to go and meet him when the plane struck the Pentagon. The place where we had arranged to meet was the very spot where it impacted and killed my boss's boss. For whatever reason, I was still at my desk but knocked to the ground. I stood up. The sprinklers above our heads started to go off and I looked around the corner to make sure all the people who worked for me were okay. I remember looking in particular at this one lady who said in a strong tone of voice. "Get out of here now." On that floor alone, nearly 27 people lost their lives. Those who had been sitting just ten yards to the right of my floor were also killed.'

Lt Col. Cleary knew instinctively that fleeing the building would be ill-advised, even though he had to make off from the impact. Assisting the woman and others away from the crash scene, he moved out to the fourth corridor. But the fire doors had already started dropping. With support, he helped people get out but had to go back into the Pentagon to make sure nobody else was hurt or stranded. There was an atmosphere of confusion because, at that point, they did not know it was a plane that had struck the building. They tried to return to their work area but could not get near.

'As we went in there, this impenetrable wall of black smoke was rolling forward on top of us,' he recalled. 'We tried to go in a little further but realised we couldn't. We stood as close as we could. We started yelling for people and listening. What was most overwhelming was the absolute lack of sound. I later realised the fire was burning all the oxygen and was just being sucked out. I stood there a little while to see if we could hear anybody or detect any movement. There was absolute dead silence. We moved back out to the corridor and saw that the doors had collapsed down as fire barriers.'

Lt Col. Cleary said that, at that moment, he noticed a colleague, who had sustained serious burns, walking down the hall from the E ring of the Pentagon and collapsing in front of them. 'We picked him up by his back without realising most of the burns were actually on his back. We were getting flesh and burnt clothes on our hands.' They carried him through storm doors, an office, down through flights of stairs and ended up in the most interior ring of the Pentagon.

PRELUDE

That day proved also to be a spiritual watershed for Thomas Cleary. When his father died from cancer two years earlier, he had started to doubt his beliefs. Now, after the events of 9/11, he found his faith being slowly rekindled. 'I have come full circle and my faith has been deepened. My time didn't happen that time. I could have been right where the impact happened. That plane could have hit one degree to the right. It could have done any number of things and I wouldn't be here.' It seemed all the more miraculous because his wife had just given birth to a child they had been trying to conceive for a long while. The baby was just three weeks old on the day of the terrorist attacks.

But for Anne McHugh, who worked on the eighty-fourth floor of Tower Two at the World Trade Center, there was to be no such jubilation. As the building crumbled, Anne instinctively put others before herself and did not survive. I learned about Anne's courage from a man who knew her better than most – her fiancé, Patrick Day, a designer of museum exhibits at New York's public library. The atrocities had erupted at a watershed in the couple's lives.

'We were going to be married,' Patrick told me. 'We had planned the wedding for 24 November 2001, in Florence, Italy. All the documents had been signed and stamped. Everything was with the priest. The date had been specially arranged so it did not clash with any crucial New York Yankees' matches. Through the events of 9/11, my faith was deepened and severely tested at the same time.'

Patrick described how, the evening before the attacks, he had held a bachelor party with friends – the American equivalent of the British stag night. The best man had slept on the couch in the couple's apartment, so the next morning Anne and Patrick had made as little sound as possible as they got ready for work. Patrick remembered giving her a kiss before she hailed the elevator and went off to work at Euro Brokers where she was vice-president on the agency bond desk. When he had eventually reached his office forty blocks away,

WATERSHED

he had called her at the World Trade Center because she had been teasing him about not falling back to sleep and not getting to work in time after the party. He had attempted to get to the office early but ended up arriving ten minutes late. So he had phoned to tell her that he had made it and they had chatted for nearly half an hour.

'I was on the phone with her when the first plane hit Tower One,' Patrick went on. 'Anne said to me, "Something's hit the building. There's stuff everywhere. I have to go." She said it so fast and hung up the phone. I rang right back and asked for Anne. A man said, "I think she's off the desk." I rang back again. I wanted to speak to someone who knew her. I got her friend who told me not to worry. It wasn't Tower Two. It was Tower One. They were fine. He said he thought Annie had left for the day. We laughed because we were just about to get married and Day is my last name. They used to laugh when I rang up because she would be "Annie Day" when we got married. "Annie day now," they'd joke. "Annie day now".'

'When I was talking to her on the phone that morning, everyone ran outside to see the explosion but I stayed at my desk. I called back again. All the guys said she had left. Her building hadn't been hit at that point. But I was worried. I had started getting calls from back home in Ireland and from my parents as well. Everybody was worried about Anne. I was waiting for her to get outside and call me.'

Patrick learned that friends of the couple had left the office after her, but had still succeeded in escaping from the crumbling tower. Some even said they could not have managed this without Anne who had helped them find their way out when they were nervous and confused. After the memorial service for the victims of 9/11, people Patrick had never met came up to him, pointed at Anne's picture and said they would never have got out alive without the selfless bravery of this young woman. They did not even know her name but she remained in their memory. Anne was the type of person who would have stopped to help people. But it was not her first experience of

PRELUDE

being on the receiving end of a terrorist atrocity. She had been working at the World Trade Center – in the office of Canada in Tower One – in 1993 when the first bombing there had taken place. She had walked down 107 narrow flights of stairs that day in the dark with the billowing smoke around her.

'We were very well suited for one another,' said Patrick. 'We had waited a long time to meet each other. Even though I miss her, I wouldn't trade places with anybody in the world for having had that experience of having her in my life. I still feel she is part of it. I look forward to when we're together again in the next life. I really do feel we will be.'

Patrick told me he always carried at least one picture of Anne with him. He showed me the photograph of his smiling fiancée, along with a picture of her as a baby and a piece of her hair. They had been so happy, he said. But it was important to remember how blessed they had been to find each other. Some people had never tasted a day of the kind of happiness they had shared.

Sometimes he woke up in the middle of the night and wondered why. He could not bear to sleep in their bed by himself so he had bought a gigantic pillow to place on Anne's side of the mattress. 'I always had to climb over her if I was getting up first, so I had to put a pillow there in her spot,' he said. 'Somehow that empty space in the bed broke my heart more than having that big pillow there. I know it's not Anne. But I couldn't stand climbing on to my side of the bed without having to climb over something. That pillow makes it easier to sleep. There are times I do wake up having nightmares. I am in the building trying to find her or looking through the rubble. When I go to bed at night I hope that, even if I have some nightmares, I will also have a dream where we're together. I know we will be one day.'

He added movingly but without sentimentality, 'Even if I went out to mail something, I would always blow a kiss to Anne in the towers. When I walked back to our apartment after the attacks on 9/11, I still blew a kiss, even though the building had fallen.'

Few experience such irruptive events in the course of their lives but the vivid recollections of Thomas Cleary and Patrick Day seemed to me to illustrate how faith can both survive and grow through unthinkable calamity. Christian belief for Thomas deepened out of a sense of humility and thankfulness that his life had been spared. While he could not reason what had happened, he was nonetheless able to articulate a feeling of gratitude which accompanied a reigniting of his faith. For Patrick, still shaken by his personal tragedy, acceptance of his loss became a hallmark of his onward spiritual journey, even though what had been taken from him remained at a level of incomprehension and mystery. The precision and clarity of their accounts have stayed with me for more than a decade. Watersheds often come upon us without warning but, as I discovered that evening in New York, holding onto faith in extreme circumstances is not an impossibility.

Such stories motivated this book in which we hear from an extraordinary range of women and men, many of whom have reached new levels of self-understanding after living through their particular crisis – or series of them. It is perhaps not without significance that many of those profiled have a close association with the arts, which have long inspired people towards moral and spiritual growth as well as the education of feeling.

A well-known television dance judge on both sides of the Atlantic describes how he uprooted himself from his native Italy in order to become the person he felt he was meant to be. I spend a few days on the East Coast of the United States with a one-time Hollywood star who is now a Benedictine prioress, while two child actors from post-war British cinema unveil their subsequent lives away from the big screen

A Catholic woman in Florida talks about the evening she was

PRELUDE

attacked in her home and left for dead by someone she knew. I hear from a former soldier in the Balkans who moved to Britain to become a Hindu monk. An ex-heroin addict tells me how, in desperation, he flung himself on a cathedral altar and begged God to change his life, and a father in Northern Ireland recalls how his life changed after his son was killed in a terrorist explosion.

I hope these stories, told to me as I was moving towards a spiritual watershed of my own, will inspire you to face your own turning points with courage and creativity - to keep on the road especially when you feel like giving up or branching off, for perseverance is the test of any journey of faith. Indeed, Jesus tells his disciples, 'Your endurance will win you your lives' (Luke 21:19).

As I discovered, through these path-crossings – and at my own turning point – a watershed is not so much a state of transition as a process of transformation.

CHAPTER ONE
CHOICE AND COST

Foreign correspondents often end up in conflict zones but my journalistic travels have often taken me into a different kind of battleground. Monasteries are places where women and men engage, not in contemplative niceties, but in spiritual warfare. Thomas Merton saw it as a life of hope and hardship, risk and penance, outer renunciation and inner revolution. For him, working out our identity in God was a labour that required sacrifice, risk and tear-filled anguish.

Although intrigued by the monastic life and constantly nourished by the writings that emerge from it, I know that I do not have the makings of a monk (at least not for more than a few days). It may well be an attraction of opposites but, whenever I've been on an assignment, I've always checked out the nearest monastery – if only on a map. For example, when I was reporting on the run-up to the Hong Kong handover, I took a boat to the spiritual haven that is Lantau Island in the South China Sea. Located at the mouth of the Pearl River, the 'island of prayer' is home to many monasteries, including Our Lady of Joy, owned by the Trappists, and Po Lin, which has the world's largest bronze Buddha statue, known as Big Buddha.

Likewise, on a research trip to New Mexico, I made my way 13 miles down a dirt road off a highway and into the Chama River Canyon where, according to Merton, the church at the Monastery of Christ in the Desert fits perfectly in its setting. Stark, lonely, stately in its simplicity, he tells us, it gazes out over the sparse fields into the widening valley. The tower is like a watchman looking for something or someone of whom it does not speak.

Monasteries are places we visit to readjust our perspective. For

CHOICE AND COST

the late film director Anthony Minghella (who bore a passing resemblance to Merton) Quarr Abbey, on his native Isle of Wight, was a spiritual health farm, a place of refreshment from gruelling work schedules and constant travel. It provided rules, routine and order – the antithesis of the chaos and madness of movie-making. 'I think all film-makers work some way towards architecture and music – the two elements of Quarr I love most,' he told me in an interview for BBC Radio 4. 'In music and architecture I am most obsessed by form and function.' In the simplicity of its form, the assertion of use over uselessness and that of function 'over a kind of careless beauty', the Benedictine abbey offered him 'a glimpse of what one could be like but isn't'.

It was, Minghella conjectured, daunting to imagine and understand that the abbot and his monks lived like that all the time. I had often thought the same as I spoke with monks and nuns about the cost of making a life-changing decision – no more so than when I flew to America to meet a former Hollywood actress who had made her name in films with Elvis Presley before becoming a Benedictine prioress.[2]

PERFORMANCE AND TRUTH

I arranged a rendezvous with Mother Dolores in New York City – but not at one of the Broadway theatres where she had once performed. We shook hands in a medical suite on Madison Avenue where she was attached to a drip as she underwent fortnightly treatment for peripheral idiopathic neuropathy disorder, a painful condition which affects many Americans. After the consultation, we moved out into Manhattan and drove past stage doors she had known in the late 1950s. 'I was just turning 20 years when I had this remarkable break,' she said, confessing that she had been 'very dewy-eyed about everything' in believing she could handle her new world. 'I'm not so sure I would feel the same way today. I think that

WATERSHED

youth has the wonderful advantage of being quite unintelligent about the difficulty of living.'

As she glanced through the car window, I asked if she could remember experiencing any unease about joining the acting profession. She replied that she had had 'more of a dis-ease' with the Catholic Church. 'When I became an actress, a priest told me that I should leave the industry because it was an occasion of sin. That nearly blew my mind. I thought it was the most ridiculous, stupid thing I had ever heard in my life.' She knew the profession was likely to be sleazy at one level but valuable at others.

Dolores Hart told me how she had been born in Chicago 'to my mother and grandmother as two mothers because my mother was 16 when I was conceived and my grandmother immediately took me on, thinking that my mother was too young.' So she had become her mother's and her grandmother's child. Although drawn to Catholicism in childhood, it was showbusiness than ran through her veins. Her father was a film actor in Hollywood, her uncle was the opera singer Mario Lanza and her grandfather was a cinema projectionist. The acting abilities and natural beauty of young Dolores impressed a talent scout and, at 18, she landed a contract to play opposite Elvis Presley in the film *Loving You*. Dolores had, in fact, never heard of Elvis but, when she told girl friends, they fainted with joy. It was indeed to prove a watershed. I listened intently as she described her first meeting with the king of rock 'n' roll.

'We went in and Elvis was sitting on the chair across from me. He immediately jumped to his feet and was as much the gentleman as anyone I have ever met before or since in Hollywood. He couldn't have been more sweet, and was very loving in his attitude. He wanted to be very solicitous. But he wasn't pushy or anything. The story is true that I was the one who gave – well maybe, it was Elvis who gave me or I gave him – we gave one another our first screen

CHOICE AND COST

kiss. I remember Elvis as quite light and joyful and a fun-loving boy who did not yet have the burden of the many late-night overtures of thousands and thousands of songs on him and whatever medical problems were being given to him in abuse and whatever kinds of things were thrown at him after his mother's death. I am sorry that he had to bear this.'

But although Dolores relished her life as an actress, something deeper had been stirring. She had already begun making retreats to the Abbey of Regina Laudis in Bethlehem, Connecticut, and had come to realise that, eventually, she would have to make an important decision. 'I had been in motion pictures for seven years when I was called by the Lord to become a Benedictine nun and that may seem very surprising to some but it was more of a surprise for me,' she told me.

In June 1963, at the age of 25, she took a taxi cab to the monastery for the latest of a number of visits. On this occasion she came to test her vocation as a postulant – attached to the community but not yet a full member of it. Dolores explained how she prayed that she would be told by God to go back and forget about the calling. 'I wanted this hound of heaven to cease but the inner voice that kept urging me to stay at Regina Laudis to pursue this vocation was something that I couldn't resist. I really didn't want this vocation but it wasn't something that was a human decision. It was truly God's call and I knew that. Eventually I knew that wasn't something that was my desire.'

The divine invitation meant that Dolores Hart would not only have to relinquish her cinematic career but also turn her back on marriage. Becoming a nun meant abandoning a relationship with her fiancé, Don. A month after their engagement they had held a party but Don noticed that Dolores had seemed not to be present. Her thoughts had been elsewhere. On the way home Don asked Dolores if she loved him. Dolores tried to assure him but Don was not convinced. The conversation upset the actress and she went off on another retreat to think things through.

The Mother Abbess at the community asked Dolores what she wanted – and also what was in her heart. She responded by saying she needed clarification as to whether she was truly called by God to be a nun. The Abbess asked again, 'What do you want Dolores?' Came the reply, 'I want to do what God wants. But I want California and to marry Don.' The Reverend Mother posed the question three times and Dolores conceded that she willed what God willed.

After passing through the watershed and eventually entering the order, Dolores said she wrestled not so much with whether or not she had made the right decision but with whether or not she could handle what was being asked of her through it. The demands of the life of a cloister were somewhat different from the privileges of being a Hollywood glamour girl. 'For the first seven years, I cried myself to sleep every night,' she told me. 'It was not easy because one may have a vocation but one has to work at it. You have to find in your own heart the meaning of what you have done. No one could possibly understand very easily what it costs to make that choice. My fiancé was wonderful in his capacity to accept what the Lord had asked of me and I truly feel he was a prince in his capacity to accept my decision. We are still friends.

'I don't think that I felt I was turning my back on Hollywood. I felt that I had to go into a deeper experience of something. I left licence to gain freedom. People think something is free, yet what they have is licence. Eventually you discover freedom as something very different from what you thought. Freedom is a matter of the heart. It is not a matter of doing what you want to do at any time you want to do it.'

Mother Dolores defined the verb 'to act' as 'to do – and to constantly do what needs to be done'. The lesson she had learned from the community's foundress was that no matter how you feel,

CHOICE AND COST

even if you have a bodily temperature of 102 degrees, you still go on the stage of the world you are in. 'I think that is the greatest lesson one can learn as a nun: no matter how you feel, your sentiments or your own sentimentality don't get in your way. You do what needs to be done for another. It's not so much of a discipline as the discipline that lends to love. Discipline for the sake of discipline is vanity but a discipline that is a strength, that is for love. It is a givenness in truth for another reason.'

Yet entering the order did not signal the credits to her life on the stage. With the help of such Hollywood stars as Paul Newman and Patricia Neal, she built an open-air theatre in the grounds of the 400-acre monastery with woodlands as the backdrop. She also set up her own production company initiating annual musicals though not performing herself. As she showed me around in the searing heat of a July morning, passing a studio chair with the words 'Mother Dolores' on the back, she explained: 'I really wanted to have a theatre here because I think St Benedict would have wanted to advance the notion that theatre was always something in the heart of the liturgy. I think the monastic theatre brings a true holiness to the art form. They used to have plays before matins so that the idiots who couldn't understand the Latin would know what was going on. I am still one of the idiots who needs plays to understand.'

I asked Mother Dolores whether she felt her two realms – the theatrical and the monastic – came together through the open-air theatre or, at the end of the day, was it all one world? She replied that it was, to her, one world because the players, musicians and skilled workers brought their gifts to bear in the theatre with a holiness that was the best of themselves. 'That is all that God is. The best of who we are.

'It has been a great satisfaction to me to realise that God called me to be here and to find the persons here that were important to Hollywood so they would have a context that would be meaningful to them. Our chaplain is also our musician and musical conductor in our plays, so is he a chaplain or is he a musical conductor? He is both and he is also someone who brings to bear a co-ordinated truth of holiness for people who come and see that there is a left hand and right hand that works in both ways. That goes for each nun in my community who has held a professional role in the world.

'I think we are always performing. I think performance has a different meaning from per-form. It's more of an enriching word. We start out in life thinking of performance as an outer shell, something that we do that is apart from our inner capacity. Later we discover that to per-form is to perfect what is form in us. It's to correct a form that is truly our own inner truth. I think doubts are part of our struggles as humans. I remember being so touched by the story of Pope Paul when he died. The very last day he prayed for the gift of endurance that he would not fail God in the last hour. We must always ask for the gift of faith because it is a gift. It is not something we can demand, that we can conjure up or that we can create out of our human capacity to trick ourselves. It is a gift.'

Mother Dolores said she was grateful still to be a full member of the Motion Picture Academy, the only nun voting for the Oscars. She said she believed in the Benedictine discipline of *lectio divina*, to read the word. 'The Word of God comes to us in many different ways and I think that motion pictures are a modern way of reading,' she said. 'It's reading the viewpoint of what is happening through the art of film. It's saying what is going on in the culture through films.'

I asked if she felt her life would have been incomplete if she had been an actress who had not embraced the monastic or if she had been a nun who had never embraced the theatrical? 'I probably would have been suicidal on either ends of it – I'm serious. I don't think that you can divorce yourself from who you are. I think that you have to marry your self and, if you try to be a nun without the truth of your whole being or an actress without the fullness of your spiritu-

CHOICE AND COST

ality, you're kidding yourself. You have to live to the fullness of the gift that God has brought in you – and that you have to explore. You explore that in prayer – and prayer tells you what the next step is going to be.'

SILENCE AND DESIRE

Back in England, another American contemplative had been on my journalistic 'Wanted' list for years. I had read all her books but one of them in particular had stayed with me – perhaps because I recognised some truths within its thesis. *Pillars of Flame* by Maggie Ross critiques institutional power in the church to devastating effect. 'No one, man or woman, has a right to ordination, and ordination does not bestow the humility of Christ, which is priesthood.'[3] On several occasions, Ross (aka Sister Martha Reeves) had been approached about ordination but had always refused, believing that her vocation was to Christ's priesthood in her being and not to function as part of an ordained secular power structure.

Much of what she lambasts about the hierarchical nature of ministry (and those clergy who seek to control) I had witnessed from time to time in both my work as a journalist and in my life as a Christian – the power trips, the manipulation, the sexism, the arrogance and the affectation. Of course, you find all that in the media too. But I had observed also the humility, compassion, sacramental joy and sacrificial love of many ordained women and men who did not fit the mould of the ambitious cleric.

Introducing herself as Martha, the theologian met me in a hotel bar in Oxford enhanced by photographs of the cast from *Morse*. It was the perfect place to ruminate on the mysteries of vocation. 'A lot of people who have been ordained, thinking it would facilitate their contemplative life, have been sadly disappointed—and in some cases completely destroyed. I believe the system has degenerated to the point that ordination is spiritual suicide.'

WATERSHED

I asked her to elaborate. 'Ordained people seem to withdraw from their own humanity by artifice, by fulfilling a set of clerical stereotypes and projections inflicted on them by institution and laity alike,' she went on. 'The problem is that if someone withdraws from their humanity in the service of the church they're saying that Christianity is not a religion of the incarnation – and something not of this world. They are saying that to relate to God you have to reject what God has created and called good – and through which God engages the world. This observation is not popular among the clergy but it is an honest view. Something dreadful seems to happen to people when they are ordained.'

Martha believes we need to jettison the word 'priest'. She reminds me that Jesus spent his entire ministry challenging the priesthood of the temple. 'You can behold,' he says to his disciples in John 14, but the system cannot behold. And because it cannot behold, it cannot receive the spirit of truth. In Martha's view (and in that of the Austrian-born, Jewish philosopher Martin Buber), Jesus wanted to return to a pre-Law Judaism to restore what she is beginning to think was a silence tradition once essential to Judaism. But it was suppressed in much the same way as Christianity. The key to this view is the word 'behold': the Law is given only because the people refuse to behold. In Genesis 1:29, behold (*hinneh*) signals the first word of the ur-covenant, and its occurrence (*idou*) in the final verse of Matthew signals the first word of the new covenant, the new creation. Sadly, she points out, modern translations have, for the most part, eliminated the word, which occurs more than 1,300 times in the ancient languages. Its disappearance has drastically changed both meaning and theology in the Bible – for the worse.

For Martha, Philippians 2:5–11 is the model for priesthood: 'He emptied himself, taking the form of a servant.' She notes that it was only by becoming completely empty of self-serving that Jesus could be exalted. 'His self-emptying creates what I call a space of

CHOICE AND COST

opportunity,' she tells me. 'He emptied himself out of pure love – there was no guarantee that God would exalt him. And as the Letter to the Hebrews says, it is only because he is a layman and not of the priestly tribe that he can be high priest. Jesus was a person; Christ is a process. Jesus came to show us this process; his en-Christing is the consequence of his undistracted beholding.'

Martha Reeves was professed as a solitary in 1980. 'I really didn't have any choice,' she said. 'Something happened to me when I was five years old that determined the course of my life; and when I returned to myself, as it were, I knew from the residual effect that whatever it was I had encountered in the absence, out of my own sight, was what I wanted to give my life to. At least this was what I said to myself in some wordless way. At the time I knew nothing about religion nor had I ever before been in a church. Fortunately I already knew that I should not try to speak of what had occurred to anyone. I would have liked – and tried very hard – to live an ordinary life but it simply wasn't to be.

'I am wary of words such as "vocation" that we toss around so glibly. Too often this word implies that God has a will and it's like a railway track. You must force the little car onto it so that it runs only on the rails. The word is also used as a way of trying to give validity to selfish agendas. I don't think the railway model is the way God works at all. As Einstein noted, there are many futures. My life has the same kind of mystery that every life has. We don't ever really know – we can't know because of the way we are made – what is our own truth, which unfolds out of our sight. Other people can sometimes observe part of our truth better than we can. In the end we can only open our empty hands and hope: "I did what I could by the light that I had." And I don't think anything is wasted, especially not our sins and failures.

'As I have grown into what was given to me – or, to put this another way, as it has unfolded in the circumstances of my life – it

WATERSHED

has, in the end, with my consent, imperceptibly taken over my life. It has, in addition, shown me how utterly countercultural the life of a solitary is. From my point of view, my life is conventional and commonsensical; from other points of view, it arouses curiosity, amusement, contempt or fear, sometimes all four at once, because I'm not interested in being out there Christmas shopping, or going out drinking or dancing my head off every night, or filling my ears with noise all day. I love to dance, and music is essential – but only as they emerge spontaneously now and again from the silence.

'Being a solitary isn't what a person does; it's who they are. It is possible to introduce a restless and unhappy individual into a space they might normally avoid or don't know exists, to their great benefit. But the consumer culture makes people afraid of silence. It implies that desiring to be alone is abnormal or maladaptive, when in fact it is essential to the way human beings evolved, and bears within it the source of our life, health and peace. Silence is our natural state, but to recover our humanity, people have to choose to engage it.'

At the time of our conversation, Maggie Ross was completing her new book on silence.[4] As she talked, she sometimes used analogies to reflect her life as a solitary in Alaska, an environment where one must give up one's own agenda or die. She compared living in the wilderness to the journey into interior silence. In both, all of one's subtle senses came alive. In Alaska, her skin told her about humidity and barometric pressure, while her nose and ears gathered information she might not be able consciously to recognise or name to herself. She was once picking blueberries on one side of a clump of bushes when the hair went up on the back of her neck. Even though she wasn't able to see, even smell anything unusual, or have any other empirical knowledge of why this was happening, she had learned to pay attention. She knew there was a bear on the opposite side of the berry patch, and backed away quickly and quietly.

CHOICE AND COST

Entering the spiritual life, she explained, requires a sensitivity similar to what is needed for picking berries in bear country, except that preparation for the interior wilderness is precisely the opposite to that of the exterior one. To survive in the physical wilderness necessitates equipment such as a tent, water and fire-lighters. But when you enter the interior wilderness, survival demands that you take nothing at all. It requires that you strip yourself of everything, especially your ideas about silence and what you might find there. The stripping alone helps to reawaken dormant subtle senses.'

Sister Martha believes one of the main reasons we are 'in such terrible trouble' on our planet is that religious institutions have deliberately suppressed the practice of silence. From the twelfth to the fifteenth centuries, the Christian institution in the West gradually traded content for method, she claims. In other words, it discarded the knowledge it had gleaned about the mind from the dedicated practice of silence over a millennium in favour of the 'facile and empty' rhetoric of dialectic. In consequence, Christianity lost its empirical foundation; it became mere words piled on words, no longer relating to anything actual in people's lives, but only to abstract theological propositions imposed by 'a power-hungry hierarchy'. She says the meaning – the referents – of the words in the contemplative vocabulary were deliberately changed to try to prevent people from engaging the work of silence. These were doomed efforts because entering into such wisdom and practice is available to anyone who will sit in silence and solitude and observe his or her own mind, and, thankfully, she goes on, there are always a small number of people willing to undertake the task.

'It is not artifice that makes us human – quite the reverse,' she insists. 'Our lives are almost entirely artificial now, and full of the noise of artifice. The ecological crisis is in part the consequence of the loss of silence and the receptivity that is essential to silence. If we want to address this crisis, then we're going to have to learn how

WATERSHED

to listen to our core silence again. We're going to have to recover our ability to relate to our own nature in order to relate to what is left of the natural world. I think one of the reasons we are so fascinated by wildlife programmes on television is that we are watching our own lost nature – in every sense – passing before our eyes, and we realise that something is terribly, terribly wrong.

'But all is not lost. It is possible to reawaken these senses in the silence. You can take the most jaded urban dweller into the Alaska wilderness and they will wake up; you can teach anyone the first steps of the work of silence, which is meditation, and they will quickly discover the vast reaches within. Saving the planet is not an onerous task; it is participating in the joy of God. But there is very little time left, if, indeed, we have not already reached the tipping point.'

The solitary path for this theologian has been adventurous in both good and bad senses. She says the negative description most frequently applied to her has been 'intransigent', a word she takes as a compliment because spiritual maturity in part means a person who cannot be coerced. Obedience to the Gospel – any form of obedience – must be given from freedom of assent, not from coercion or dependence.

'The desire to respond to this God whose love has driven my life – this whatever that has driven my life – has never abated,' she explains. 'Even though at one level I feel I've had no choice, in the end I have made a free assent to it. It's meant quite literally letting go of everything. It's like dying, in a way; but then, we all die. We can fight our death or we can choose it. If we choose the inevitable, we make it our own, and this means that we can live our dying in the truth of who we are.'

As I learned from Mother Dolores and Sister Martha, responding to mystery is always personal. There is often an irresistibility about it, but there can also be conflict. When our

CHOICE AND COST

watershed takes the form of having to choose between rival possibilities, there is bound to be loss and gain.

The stirring is often an invitation to move closer to the truth of our being which is always being shaped in secret. We discern it, not through the competing voices of the mind, but through the wisdom of the heart. Yet once the decision has been made, we realise that the fulfilling of that vocation (if that is the word we prefer to use) may involve many more renunciations. In giving our life to something greater than ourselves and remaining faithful to that choice, we are not protecting ourselves from the spiritual darkness. We make a decision, then face its demands. The real cost of the choice might not manifest itself until much later. We may fall along the way but our sins, our failures and our reluctance to obey are never wasted.

As I weighed up the options of switching direction in my own life, I realised that any sacrificial decision would come at a price. Making a choice may lead to an immediate change in our lives. But the working out of its consequences can take a lifetime.

CHAPTER TWO
SEARCHING AND BECOMING

Harry Williams was a larger-than-life Anglican monk who joined the Community of the Resurrection in West Yorkshire after an academic career in Cambridge. An honest writer about the spiritual life and the wildernesses it can take you through, he was often in demand as a speaker. During my university days, I invited him to talk to our theological society and entertained him to lunch at a hotel across the road. It was a labyrinthine complex on several levels which we decided to explore after our meal. Absorbed in conversation, we suddenly realised we were lost in the bowels of the building and, no matter which door we tried or corridor we trod, we could not for the life of us find our way out. As the minute hand on my watch ticked dangerously close to the appointed lecture hour, we were still retracing our steps with incredulity as though being subjected to some post-prandial prank to work off the calories. I began apologising profusely to an unperturbed Father Williams who merely chuckled, 'Oh, please don't worry. I rather think I'm enjoying this.'

Finding our true spiritual identity, the person we have been created to be, is not unlike a walk around a maze or a hotel with an unfathomable infrastructure. The way ahead can be confusing, there's little in the way of route maps and we end up on false trails that draw us into cul-de-sacs. But there is no reason why it should not also be enjoyable. Going back on ourselves is all part of the adventure. It may take many years of prayer and guidance to be

SEARCHING AND BECOMING

certain we are, in fact, on track. This is all part of the process of becoming ourselves and, although there is no growth without pain, the searching need lack neither humour nor pleasure.

Harry Williams wrote a paperback on prayer called *Becoming What I Am* which was reprinted several times. In it he poses the question: how can I love my neighbour unless I am deeply aware of what I am? To become fully yourself is a terrific risk, he says, 'committing you to God knows what and leading you to God knows where'. Only absolute love, God's love, makes us fully ourselves instead of the half-people we generally are.[5]

Cornelia Connelly, who founded the Society of the Holy Child Jesus, offered similar guidance to her nuns: 'Be yourself but make that self all that God wants it to be.' But how do we really know what God intends us to be? It was a question that besieged me as I discerned a calling to leave the world of journalism.

Merton once asked, 'Why do we have to spend our lives striving to be something we would never want to be, if we only knew what we wanted? Why do we waste our time doing things which, if we only stopped to think about them, are just the opposite of what we are made for?'

These questions made a deep impact on James Martin who left the world of corporate finance to enter the Society of Jesus and, 11 years later, be ordained a priest. In his book *Becoming Who You Are*, the American writer describes how Merton's words led him to undertake a serious overview of his life.

> It was a long process, not without its doubts and confusions and frustrations and dead ends, but in the end, it seemed to me that the Jesuit way of life would be a good deal more satisfying than the corporate way of life ... It was certainly the best decision I've ever made, and, amazingly, it seemed that God had made the decision for me.[6]

WATERSHED

Becoming who we are meant to be is rarely, if ever, an overnight success story. Sometimes, on our journey towards wholeness, we need to let go of what is closest to us.

THE CHOREOGRAPHY OF FAITH

Branded 'the Italian Spitfire', international choreographer Bruno Tonioli is a charismatic judge of television dance shows on both sides of the Atlantic – *Strictly Come Dancing* in Britain and *Dancing with the Stars* in the United States. His exuberant and eloquent turns of phrase to celebrities attempting a rumba or a paso doble are themselves choreographed with animated gesticulation. Tonioli has worked extensively in the music business, choreographing videos, stage shows and tours for such music legends as Tina Turner, Sting, Elton John and the Rolling Stones.

After watching him at work on the set of *Strictly* and even being put through a quick routine with him in the bar afterwards, we met again in a coffee house near his home in North London. Away from the cameras, in dark glasses, leather jacket and jeans, Bruno seemed quieter and more reflective. Of his extroversion on screen, he simply said, 'You cannot disguise who you are. It comes naturally through you. I express myself through my Latin temperament. Sometimes I am a bit impulsive and fiery. It goes with the culture you are born in. It will never leave you and it does affect the way you live because you behave in your natural way.'

A disciplined Catholic upbringing in northern Italy had influenced him throughout his life, he confessed, though these days he distances himself from the institution of the Roman Catholic Church. An only child, he was born to poor, hardworking parents in the industrial town of Ferrara in northern Italy. His father was a bus driver, while his mother sewed upholstery for second-hand cars. They needed to work full-time and could not afford to have another child, so the young Bruno was cared for by a community of nuns.

SEARCHING AND BECOMING

'Some of them were quite strict,' he recalled. 'There was a certain discipline that you had to follow every week, such as examining your conscience and going to confession. These were the rituals that were part of Catholic Italy in the 1960s. The local priests knew everybody and there was always great respect for them. It encouraged you to rebel sometimes but it also gave you a very good sense of morality. This never leaves you, especially the sense of observing what you do. Sometimes I think the clergy were a bit too heavy on the sin side, even though they were doing it with good intentions.'

Bruno's first inclinations towards showbusiness manifested themselves when he was three. As soon as he heard music being played, he would start to dance on tables. He said he had always been aware of his natural correspondence to movement and rhythm. He loved catching American musicals in the cinema and watching his parents do the cha-cha, a dance of Cuban origin, an offshoot of the mambo. 'I always had an incredible affinity with the performing arts and I knew my future wouldn't lie in that town. My parents were not at all interested in the arts because, for them, my future would consist in working for a bank or becoming an accountant. For people who lived in that culture, that was the greatest achievement for a child. But because that wasn't me, it caused a lot of problems.

'So I made a deal with my parents that, if I got a diploma at 18, then I would leave. Learning anything about dance was very difficult in the provinces – you had to go to places like Rome. It was very hard and created a lot of conflict because my parents never understood. They had nothing in their lives to compare it with. They thought I would grow out of all the fantasies I had. But I didn't.'

As soon as he reached 18, Bruno entered a watershed as he prepared to leave the tight-knit Italian community and set about becoming the person he felt he was meant to be. That summer he met friends at an arts festival in Positano on the Amalfi coast. Later they invited him to watch a production at a prestigious theatre in

WATERSHED

Milan by the Paris-based dance company La Grande Eugene. Like the stuff of dreams, on the very day Bruno showed up, one of the performers (who happened to resemble him) decided to leave the troupe. Bruno found himself auditioning for the part of Jesus Christ, wearing an expensive attire created from glass and mirrors. 'All the clothes fitted me and they had cost a fortune. The company took a leap of faith and I took a leap of faith. I had not done anything before. I had to learn two numbers a day and, while the understudy was doing the main part, I was fed in so that, by the end of the week, I was doing the whole show. The adrenalin was such that I knew that, if I didn't go for it then, it would never happen again. I just sensed that I had to go for it.'

Bruno called his mother in Ferrara, told her he had been offered a job with a dance company in Paris and said he would not be returning. 'What do you mean you are not coming back?' came the reply. It was not an opportunity that presented itself that often to inhabitants of the Italian town, but Bruno instinctively knew he had to take hold of the reins. While the move made a great deal of sense to him, it did not to his parents. His mother was horrified. Bruno said it took years for her to come to terms with the fact that her son would not be going back home to live there permanently again.

'If I had followed the pattern my parents had laid out for me, I wouldn't be here,' said Bruno. 'There is no way I could have done this coming from my background. I literally had to upset my parents and it caused many psychological problems in the early days. It's very hard saying "I'm going. I'm leaving behind everything I know and taking a chance." There was pressure for me to conform and I had nothing to show that I was going to succeed in what I wanted to do. There were no guarantees. My mother was upset. My father was upset. They were not happy about it and it was not easy. There came a point when I had to make a decision. I left home. That was a big thing in Italy. People do not leave home, let alone go to another

SEARCHING AND BECOMING

country. For Italian mothers, it's hard, then you feel guilty. There was always the hope I would be back in six weeks or so. I had to fight my corner.'

In the early days, Bruno was able to visit his parents when he was based in Paris but, by the time he moved to London, he managed to return home just once a year at Christmas. Only when his parents eventually came to London and saw their son 'established' with his own house did they fully accept that Bruno's career as a dancer was alive and kicking. They also went to watch him perform in Germany. It was a theatrical world completely alien to them. They could not credit the fact that such a lifestyle was being embraced by their only child. It was a watershed for them as much as it was for Bruno.

Another turning point in Bruno's life came much later when, in his late thirties, his mother died at the age of 63. He then found himself living through all the guilt of not being able to be there to support her because he was working so hard. 'There is a great bond between mother and son. Even if I was away, we were always close and talked on the phone. I always felt a sense of having let her down because I wasn't there when she died. There was also a sense of guilt of having caused suffering to someone very close to you because of that. At the same time, I had to realise that, when someone loves you, the greatest suffering they can have is seeing you suffer. The fact is: my mother knew I was happy. But I went through a very long process of coming to accept the loss and facing the questions about why she had to die at a younger age than most people. The experience "detuned" me because it was very hard to come to terms with.

'To help me, I read a lot of Buddhist books such as *The Tibetan Book of Living and Dying*. I had to accept her death. I had to embrace my pain. That is easy to say but very difficult to do. It took me a few years which were really bad ones because, on top of this, a lot of my friends in the artistic world were dying of AIDS – one after another. It was like a generation being wiped out. Then my grandmother died, then my grandfather died and then a friend died of cancer. It was horrific. My friend was in her late 40s and left two daughters. Grief was constant. Every time I tried to come out of a tunnel, I had another one in front of me. This happened between 1994 and 1998. And then my father died. I couldn't take it any longer. I thought I was going to die myself.'

However, with strong feelings that he was 'protected' and had a guardian angel, Bruno Tonioli was determined neither to become resentful nor to let go of life, even though the journey ahead would at times prove daunting and traumatic. Through it, he came to a deeper acceptance of life and its vagaries. It was another turning point. Gradually he cultivated the art of emotional and psychological detachment, and thinks he is a stronger person for it. He knew he had to resolve the inner turmoil before he could move forward. He could not allow the past to haunt and unhinge him. A new decade brought fresh opportunities and new-found fame.

Although no longer a subscriber to organised religion, Bruno says he still believes in God. Faith is still necessary, especially during hard times which can assault any performer. The peak experiences of being on stage can be overshadowed by the realisation that the current success has no lifetime guarantee. Anxieties about future work can form an unsettling undercurrent in the freelance world. He says he has always had a faith that determines that he will make the right decision when doubts loom.

'You can't have faith in yourself unless you have an overall sense of mystery and of knowing that you will do the right thing,' Bruno told me. 'Faith is very important whatever form it takes. What I found irritating about organised religion was that things were repressed or suppressed, instigating hatred and doing what religion and faith should not do. The core of every religion is goodness and support,

SEARCHING AND BECOMING

about people getting the most from every moment and being in tune with each other and the world – not about disagreeing, contradicting or bringing people down. Faith is the opposite of that.'

Choreography has always been therapeutic because of the connection between creativity and human emotion. He says he responds to everything he does from an emotionally creative perspective. Nothing is externally planned; it comes from within. The arts are both a source of inspiration and an opportunity for emotional release. He is able to tap into a certain emotional state which then allows him to create. Pure emotion is associated with 'a very special part of the psyche' which enables him to express himself with relevance. Whatever he embraces can be transformed into a positive experience.

'I have never been scared of adventure, whereas most people are fearful of doing anything new or different because things can go wrong,' he said. 'I always found that the interest and excitement of a situation, and whatever I could learn out of it, overcame the fear of leaving security and a pattern of life that is set and safe. I have never felt too comfortable with the idea of a life that is planned ahead, knowing what you are going to do at every stage. Even today I almost rejuvenate when I see a big change ahead. I become totally alive. For some people, it is very hard to drop the safety net that a more ordinary way of living provides. But, in my case, I have to recognise the event when it arrives and be receptive to it.

'Like painting, singing or directing, choreography comes from within. It is innate – a vocation. You feel it inside you. When choreography works, you get this feeling of harmony. It's like a fabulous sunset or cloud. If you glimpse it once or twice, you are lucky. You feel it is pure harmony, almost like being in touch with everything. Once you have experienced that harmony, that is what you are striving for all the time. You feel it. You know that you have something there. When you go before the cameras, you hope somebody

WATERSHED

focuses on it as well. It is almost a physical response, something I can feel in my skin. You are striving, not for perfection, but for harmony when everything is in tune and works as a whole.

'When you are creating a piece, you have to have control in a theatre and on a set. You draw on the primal instincts. A spiritual or sexual experience might give you the same high. It is all eros. There is a connection because, in the Stone Age, dances were linked to mating rituals. The early forms of religion were associated with the bonding with people. From there came the Whirling Dervishes. Stylised processions in church are forms of choreography, such as the entrance of an archbishop or the pope. There is something about the ritual or procession, a mystical experience that takes people into another level of consciousness. It is all part of letting go of something to move into a different plane. Look at the Vatican. The theatricality! It is a fantastic piece of choreography. The great religious processions of Spain are a spectacle which allows people to forget everyday life and be taken away with this great glamour and beauty of the church.

'When it happens in the theatre, it can be almost hypnotic. When you structure properly, you get the audience's attention. It's like building a pyramid to the apex and, at the apex, you have this wonderful moment which leaves them spellbound. When a production is well staged, it will stay with them for ever, like a great liturgical experience. In a show, you build a sequence of events that will enhance the dramatic moment. It is like making love. It only works if that moment is real, even though it's created. You can't fake it. It is a construction, but for it to be effective it has to be believable and real. People forget they are in the theatre. It is happening in front of them for them. It is for real. The first time I received Holy Communion, I passed out, and so did three others because those people believed it. The performance was real.'

It was clear to me that, in every sense, Bruno Tonioli was his own person, a man who had become the person he was born to be.

SEARCHING AND BECOMING

But some people only discover their true selves towards the end of their lives, with no small degree of regret and resentment. Perhaps they made decisions to please others or lacked the confidence to claim who they really were. The journey towards self-fulfilment has to begin as an inner search for authenticity.

NOTES ON THE SOUL

Jelaluddin Rumi was a thirteenth-century Sufi mystic from Persia. In 2007, the Muslim was described as the most popular poet in America. It was there, in fact, that I first came across him. The singer Madonna and the actress Goldie Hawn recite Rumi's verses on a CD produced by the doctor and holistic healer Deepak Chopra. Rumi writes about union with the beloved from whom he has been cut off and become aloof. He longs to restore the relationship. His central metaphor is the reed of the flute, torn from the reed-bed. In its notes he hears the essence of nostalgia and the yearning to go home. Human speech itself, says Rumi, is like this: it longs to return to the source, as the lover desires the beloved. This sense of loss and separation lies behind both language and music.

I had once made a programme on Rumi for the BBC World Service from Bush House on the Strand in the centre of London. On my regular saunters from the studios to Westminster, I often glanced over at The Savoy, with its bowler-hatted porters urbanely opening cab doors for affluent guests. A British icon since 1889, the hotel (with its English Edwardian and Art Deco interiors) has undergone a restoration costing over £100 million. One day, when I decided to take a closer look, I could never have imagined that I was about to meet a musician who had been profoundly influenced by the Sufi sage.

'Music is my church and gave me my identity,' said the young singer in a tuxedo as I listened to him crooning the great American song book in the plush piano bar. In between medleys, Jonathan

WATERSHED

Nickoll talked about the place of Rumi in his life. Jonathan had begun his professional life selling guitars in a music store and busking on the streets of Cambridge to try to pay the rent for his room. A friend had given him a tawdry collection of Mind, Body and Spirit writings but he was far from impressed. They were far too populist for his liking. Then, one day, as he sat on the bed, flicking through the pages, he came across a quote from Rumi:

> Don't worry about saving these songs!
> And if one of our instruments breaks,
> it doesn't matter
>
> We have fallen into the place
> where everything is music.[7]

Remembering the many times he had managed to break guitar strings himself, Jonathan found himself immediately relating to the quotation. It proved to be a watershed. 'To read a sentiment to the effect that, if the physical breaks down, it does not matter because you have reached a place where music is everything, was mind-blowing,' he told me. 'That was the first time that words had touched me in the way that music had as a child. The quote influenced the next five years of my life. It was the most spiritual moment I had ever encountered.'

Jonathan owns the complete works of Rumi on recycled paper, 'which I know he would have approved of'. He says it was not uncommon for the Sufi to spend three days in an intense conversation with another person. 'I love that thought. When you put on a CD of John Coltrane or Ella Fitzgerald, listening to them is having a conversation with these people. It is timeless. With Rumi, you read his work and he is in the room with you. I have the same feeling when I listen to any performance that moves me.'

SEARCHING AND BECOMING

An initial watershed had occurred as a child when Jonathan had sensed 'almost chemical changes' occurring in his body when he realised he could play and sing. 'Apparently I was classed as a depressed child,' he said. 'I can recall feeling a bit like a spare part. When I was very young, I was slow to learn to read, slow to talk, shy and fearful. But music offered me a spiritual lifeline. I instinctively knew at the age of five that this was my destiny. I had found myself.'

A further watershed took place when he was playing with Matchbox toys on grey carpet tiles at the age of seven. The television was switched on and he became mesmerised by an Elvis Presley documentary, *That's the Way It Is*. 'The programme blew my brain,' he said. 'I suddenly felt distracted by the action on the screen. It is no hyperbole to say that my life was shaped from that very moment. I knew that's who I had to be. That's what I had to do, no question of it. It was a total epiphany in the thirty minutes before bedtime. I had something to aspire to, in essence to become as close to this universal secret that I had been let in on. Within seconds of the film finishing, I ran upstairs, grabbed a tennis racket and stood in front of a mirror. It was a lightning bolt.'

In much the same way as some people discern a vocation to priesthood while still at primary school, Jonathan felt he had been put in touch with the core of his being at that tender age. He had already discovered that music could guide him to 'another place'. His earliest memory was of hearing music and then pretending to play the piano on a pillow. But watching Elvis on the television that day was the first time he consciously thought that the die was cast for a musical career. He has since made the pilgrimage to Graceland twice and accumulated a vast collection of memorabilia including copies of Presley's 33 movies.

'I think music was innate in me,' he enthused. 'It's the only natural skill I really have. It's an inborn passion I have, a feeling for music. I have always thought it was my calling. In fact, I taught

WATERSHED

myself. My father showed me three chords on the guitar and I went crazy after that. Practice wasn't practice. It was just what I did. I listened endlessly to songs on the stereo, imitating them first with the guitar and then on the piano. Before I knew it, I had four weeks' worth of songs I could play.'

But it was in physical darkness that Jonathan nurtured his gift. From the age of six, he had an inner drive to turn off the lights in the room. This was not an obsessive–compulsive disorder but a need to be taken to that other place, a spiritual journey. He remembered pestering his parents to buy him a record player and a tape recorder. As soon as he came home from school, off would go the lights as he played his favourite music in 'a better place, an honest place'. Now in his thirties, Jonathan still heads into darkness. He admits that it is a form of catharsis as many other musicians through the ages have testified.

'It is a channel for all my pent-up emotions. Life is scary. It is a baffling and confusing world. You come home, turn the keyboard on, pick up your guitar, play and sing, and it puts things in perspective. It is an emotional release but it is also about having a conversation. If you are singing somebody else's song, for example, and conveying their lyrics, it is a communion and you feel you are part of something bigger.

'I always like to play music in the dark. It is more intense. You can't see, so you can hear better. Your senses are heightened. It is almost as though you are not alone. Some people talk about prayer that way. My form of prayer would be sitting there and singing. You tap into the universe. It is a massive experience. Your dimensions expand. You are exposed, and a harmony takes over. I regard it as a very spiritual experience. It has always been the most intense experience I have had and I have always known that I had to be part of that experience. Playing and singing are my ways of expressing that.'

SEARCHING AND BECOMING

At the same time as Jonathan was badgering his mother and father to buy him musical equipment, he also asked them to purchase a bible for him. As he was only a lad, his parents might have raised an eyebrow or two. But for Jonathan that, too, was an expression of the innate. From that early age he wanted to investigate 'what was out there, what was bigger than him'. Musicians tended to be spiritually-minded people, he pointed out, and at the age of six he seemed to be encountering the numinous through his passion for music. 'When you are sitting there playing, singing or watching someone perform, or listening to a record, you become aware of this amazing source of power in the medium. Its axis is not in the 3D world that most of us occupy. It is beyond that. So you get drawn to, want to question, and to seek out, what that spiritual world is.' And for Jonathan, 'spiritual' is a transcendent 'sense of the unknowable', a 'liberating break from logic', a space, an echo and a voice that says, "There is more. You have always sensed it. Now feel it all around you."'

Jonathan left school at 17, did A-levels at college, contemplated journalism – his father is a sub-editor on a national tabloid – but the call of the music persisted. Whenever he tried to evade the vocation, he said it tried in return to hijack him. Jonathan told me that he regarded music as a 'journey to the transcendent'. He said he had had no concept of the word 'soul' before he heard music. Whether performing or listening to great or humble music, he simply 'became aware of soul'. He stopped thinking about the tax bill and was taken somewhere else. It was identical to an inner response to an experience of wind blowing through the trees.

'I think music has put me in touch with God. I've done a lot of touring around the world with my music and have been in a lot of lonely situations on my travels around the globe, I have learnt that you certainly are not alone. With music you are never alone. You never feel alone. I always sense I have a host of spiritual

WATERSHED

companions. There have been times of great despair when I have appealed for help and help has come. It was through music that I was able to reach the spiritual realm.'

As a freelance performer, there had been times when he had been forced to face the walls of adversity. There had been little, if any, money, but at the same time great pressure from various corners for him to conform to the responsibilities of having a nine-to-five job with a regular income. That had caused him considerable strife, he admitted. Things got so bad once that he locked himself into a windowless room in a flat and turned off all the lights. In the pitch-black, he spoke out loud: 'I need some help. I need some guidance. I have no idea where I am going. Music is my life. But there are a lot of family and bank pressures on me not to carry on doing that. The hole in the wall expressed its concern by swallowing my card on numerous occasions. What do I do?'

Jonathan went on: 'It was a very, very intense experience but I was acutely aware that I was not alone in that situation. I stood there. A white light appeared behind me. It was a classic case of my nerves tingling and my hair standing on end. There was a massive presence in the room on that occasion. I wasn't told anything but I had this feeling of immense well-being and that all would be well. I encountered a spirit guide and I have had that experience since in moments of great concern, anxiety and despair.'

Music has led Jonathan into a growing self-awareness rather than introverted self-obsession. He now writes his own music which puts him directly in touch with his own feelings. Without some kind of medium or output for emotional release, it is easy, he says, to rush through life without hearing the voice of one's heart. Through music, he feels he has been put in touch with the dynamics of human complexity. 'I do not understand myself but I am self-aware, or should I say, self-amused? I have become used to myself. I am what you might call "soul-aware". I am very aware of my soul. Sometimes I

SEARCHING AND BECOMING

say to my wife, Laura, who's a cellist, "My soul aches today," and she has come to understand what I mean by that. I can have a tangible feeling of heaviness inside me. Some days my soul does feel heavy, other days it soars. Friends who are not musicians might be bemused by that concept but I think it is something you discover through performance when you are running on your soul.

'The performing arts are spiritual because their main source is something that is not physical. If you are a dancer, writer, musician or singer, the spark that ignites your fire is not tangible, so even hard-grained atheist performers must be in awe of the process from which creativity comes – far beyond our boundaries. Performing can be an incredibly spiritual experience.'

In one of his letters to a correspondent, about to make a major spiritual decision, Thomas Merton observed, 'You are, in any case, seeking to become what you already are in so many ways.'[8] The stories of Bruno Tonioli and Jonathan Nickoll are evidence that becoming one's true self is a journey that can be sensed from an early age and yet may involve several turning points along the way. Both men were touched and inspired by music as young children, an overwhelming discovery that led one to become a dancer, the other a pianist – the people they were meant to be.

But as with any authentic realisation or innate sense of one's true self, the journey towards wholeness involved searching and struggle. Much depended on each having the courage to trust 'the inner voice', to own who they were and to believe that their respective artistic worlds could offer a context for human growth and flourishing. As Catherine of Siena put it, "Be who God meant you to be and you will set the world on fire.'

CHAPTER THREE
ADDICTION AND GRACE

Each of us is probably addicted to something – chocolate, computers or a compulsion that manifests itself in the way we make the bed (or how we treat others when we get out the wrong side of it).

As I have gleaned from the books of the Christian psychiatrist Gerald May, the psychological, neurological and spiritual dynamics of full-blown addiction are creatively at work within each human being. The same processes accountable for addiction to narcotics and alcohol are also responsible for addictive ideas, work patterns, relationships, power crazes, fame obsessions, and fantasies of every kind.

Although addictions are part and parcel of how we operate, they are also our own worst enemies. Gerald May makes the point that they enslave us with chains of our own making and yet are virtually beyond our control. Addiction makes idolaters of us all because it compels us to worship the objects to which we are fatally attached. Addiction is 'at once an inherent part of our nature and an antagonist of our nature. It is the absolute enemy of human freedom, the antipathy of love. Yet, in still another paradox, our addictions can lead us to a deep appreciation of grace. They can bring us to our knees.'[9]

These insightful remarks, from a doctor who spent many years listening to the yearnings of other people's hearts, were much on my mind as I drove into the Sefton Park area of Liverpool to meet a 35-year-old doctoral student whose tough journey from personal disintegration to self-empowerment had undoubtedly taken its toll. But as we hastily climbed the stairs to his bedsit, engaging in pleasantries across parallel bannisters, it was difficult to imagine that the articulate and intelligent postgraduate leaping ahead of me was actually a former heroin addict who had spent thirteen years in what he described as a hell of his own making.

THE CRUSHING OF THE SELF

Between the ages of 16 and 29, Stephen fed a habit whose diet comprised of cannabis, ecstasy, LSD, amphetamines, magic mushrooms, cocaine, methadone, heroin, crack cocaine and tranquillisers. It was a costly addiction and, to pay for it, he turned shoplifter and impersonated doctors to wheedle prescriptions. The addiction even led to his being subject to extreme violence and terror. But it was not the dramatic episodes he remembered most vividly but the crushing sameness of everyday, knowing he needed to 'graft' – obtain money for the drugs his body was screaming out for and seek out another dark corner where he could 'shoot up' in private.

Stephen's watershed moment came in 2003 when 'something deep inside' snapped and he was starkly confronted with his utter poverty. The road to recovery through detox and rehab was slow and painful, but he managed to address the issues of self-hatred that had driven him to drugs. What was more, he had gained a double first in theology and started working on a PhD about addiction and spirituality. He even began lecturing at his university and worked with families affected by substance abuse. In contrast to his former existence, Stephen said he was now leading a life of overflowing fullness, brimming with wonder and excitement. 'I was waiting to die and couldn't hope for myself,' he told me. 'But it was enough that others hoped for me. Now I have come alive again.'

I was curious to hear more because I knew that Stephen had

WATERSHED

been born into a well-respected family. He had not come from a background of social deprivation and unemployment, sometimes associated with drug addiction. As he talked quickly and openly, Stephen disclosed how he had been a deeply troubled child who had felt isolated from the rest of the family but had also sensed he was a person of intense creative energy.

'The discovery of drugs was actually a semi-religious experience with altered states of consciousness, and I got into this in a big way,' Stephen revealed. 'I was a chronic dope smoker for many years, dropped out of university after a year and wanted to concentrate on my life as a musician, which included some television work. But my addiction overshadowed all that. I would steal just to buy cannabis. Then I crashed into this huge depression. I took more and more dope, and even made a couple of suicide attempts. At one point I ended up in a coma for a week. These were not cries for help but really serious attempts to end my life. I wanted out. I didn't like my life and I hated myself.'

Cannabis, ecstasy and LSD became forms of escape from the memories of childhood. Stephen's first depression reared its head after he had been using the heroin substitute, methadone. Just ten milligrams unlocked the elixir of life, evaporating the pain, self-hatred, anxiety and tensions into sensations of warmth, peace and tranquillity. He knew about the lethal power of heroin and opiates but could not resist. Crack cocaine followed. He could maintain a heroin habit on £20–30 a day but the insatiability of crack cocaine could cost £500 a day. At one point Stephen was spending two hundred pounds a day on crack and having to shoplift. And it went on for years, between the ages of 24 and 29, even resulting in his becoming involved in life-threatening situations. Such hair-raising episodes convinced him that the more someone is entrenched in addiction, the rational option of quitting is simply not on the radar. The only way out is to take more drugs to escape the painful reality.

ADDICTION AND GRACE

The prolonged use of crack can spiral into paranoia but Stephen's main drug of choice was always heroin, about which he has lucid recall. Withdrawal induced 'a sense of unreality and a very hellish state'.

Stephen told me that addiction derived from a Latin legal term meaning 'a court-imposed giving of oneself to another master or surrendering oneself to another master'. And Stephen had surrendered himself to the master called heroin. Crack use became occasional when he could afford it. The drugs numbed, faded, blocked out and pushed into the background inner feelings he could not face. But the deep emotional tensions hung around, driving and coaxing him to keep taking the drugs. Heroin addiction, he pointed out, was not proverbial rocket science. Heroin (a chemical called diamorphine) is a painkiller and that was precisely what it did. Someone in deep existential pain, finding this drug, would regard it as a blessing, he said.

Stephen's turning point came at a time when his life was completely out of control. Arrested for shoplifting, he started to munch 300 valium tablets from an illegally obtained bottle. He says he existed in a semi-conscious stupor for two weeks, yet still managed to maintain his habit. Stephen has few memories of this period, except the recollection of waking up in police cells for two weeks. Yet even after this custodial routine, he still managed to maintain his habit. Eventually the police rolled all Stephen's charges into one and, on the day of sentencing, he braced himself for a period behind bars.

'I had been given other chances through probation but had messed them up,' he went on. 'I was very scared. I was sitting in the court waiting room. My father was there. I was assigned a court solicitor whom I found quite insulting. He said I was a junkie. He was professional but there was an undercurrent of loathing and hatred. He asked what I was doing with my life. I had A-levels and

WATERSHED

had come from a good family. He said he could stop me from going to prison if, as an alternative, I allowed him to get me a drug treatment and testing order. He said he could get me out of going to prison, but only if I would tell him that I would do whatever it takes to turn my life around.

'He gave me a few minutes to think about it. All of a sudden I became hyperaware of my situation. I could smell the stench of my body. I didn't wash. I had sweaty clothes. I was so intoxicated on tranquillisers and heroin, I could not even hold my head up. I was slumped in my seat and just became aware of the poverty of my situation, of the utter destitution I was in. I had been in and out of hostels and had had these experiences with all kinds of stuff. In that moment, it all seemed to come together in the words of the young solicitor. I emerged from this fog of intoxication and, in a moment of clarity or pseudo-clarity, something very deep inside me snapped and I thought, "I have had enough of this." I was 29.' He came back. I told him, "Yes, I will do whatever it takes." Those words – the depth of that commitment – have carried me through some of the toughest times of my recovery.

The order was granted and shouldered Stephen through all the difficulties ahead. He had to report to a probation officer every day and undertake a drug test twice a week. Reports had to be written every month and he had to attend tightly controlled courses. He obtained a prescription for Subutex, then a new alternative to methadone, an opiate replacement, and that was the beginning of a new direction. But it was a slow recovery. There were times when he lapsed. After nine months, Stephen needed to be weaned off the Subutex as an in-patient at a detox unit. This entailed the medical flushing out of the intoxicants in his system. Rehab is a longer-term process where the addict addresses in a therapeutic environment the issues that led to his or her drug use. This was where, according to Stephen, the deep healing later took place.

ADDICTION AND GRACE

Stephen had been brought up a Catholic. Even though he believed himself to be a spiritual person, religion troubled him. As a young child he had wanted to be a monk. There was a period in his drug addiction when he entered a series of exchanges with the Cistercian monastery of Mount St Bernard in Leicestershire. After a series of retreats, he went to live with the community for three months. He thought that was where God wanted him to be. It was an intense experience. There he detoxed himself but had not addressed any of the underlying issues. He managed to come off drugs and started to grow in this safer environment. The abbot even told him, 'We'll accept you as a novice if you go away for six months, tie up all your loose ends and then come back.'

But within two days of returning to Manchester, Stephen was back on heroin.

'That is how much of a hold it has on you if you don't sort out some of the stuff that drives it,' Stephen said. 'Even deeper than this visceral sense of belonging in the monastery were those unresolved knots of pain, tensions and issues that were still lurking. They may have been silent for a bit during my period there but they were still there as I found out when I came home.'

Stephen found rehabilitation hugely challenging as he worked through the issues. That is where, he told me, he was transformed from the addict to the person who was no longer an addict. In contrast to the 12-step spiritual approach of Alcoholics Anonymous, where he would have said, 'My name is Stephen. I am an addict,' he did not desire an explicitly religious context for his recovery. He said he felt that God had made his life complex enough so he did not want God to be involved. Furthermore, Stephen wanted to be responsible for his own recovery, 'not some supernatural being I felt increasingly distant from'. He chose instead a therapeutic community because it did not have a religious ethos and, crucially, claimed that it would transform him

WATERSHED

from an addict into someone else. That happened after nine long months.

Stephen said that in rehab it was possible to come close to people beyond the margins of society, such as girls who had been involved in prostitution since the age of 12 or other people 'beaten and utterly broken, completely disenfranchised from mainstream society'. Without fail, he told me, each had a heart as big as the universe with such creativity and spirit. It was only later that he had the feeling that it would make sense to share some of his struggles for the benefit of others. He became an undergraduate and, although he has continued to suffer bouts of serious illness, he has not looked back. His doctoral thesis is entitled, 'From addict self to spiritual self: spiritual technologies of recovery in the theology of addiction'.

Recovering addicts often describe their journeys in profoundly spiritual terms. Intractable addiction, said Stephen, was a spiritual state, a sense of absence – of God and of wholeness. 'There is no other state so utterly antithetical to what is whole and spiritual than the addict. Even as an addict in hostels, I would have rosary beads and plead with God. I have thrown myself on altars. This happened at Salford Cathedral where I cried, "Please help me. Save me." I read some of the psalms such as "Out of the depths I cry to you ...." Addicts can say those words with a depth of feeling that few others are able to. Each word resonates so profoundly with the addict. It's a process of development. The spiritual self exists in the addict as a potential and is somehow developed in recovery.

'There is always hope. During the latter stage of my drug-abuse career, I was waiting to die. At one point my mum came to meet me with some sandwiches. She held my hand and said, "I know you are going to get through this Stephen." I couldn't believe it. I couldn't hope for myself. Sometimes someone else hoping for you is enough to carry you through – someone else believing in you, someone else hoping in you.

ADDICTION AND GRACE

'Hope for them because that is enough. Society's hope is enough to carry people through.

'I love myself now, and my life. I am so at peace and happy. That is not to say that life isn't difficult but I have learnt how to live life. In rehab I confronted the enemy within and started to explore some of the issues of my childhood. It doesn't work for everyone. It doesn't have a high success rate. But for me it has been a journey from darkness to light, from brokenness to wholeness, from fracture to oneness and a state of integration, from being on the margins to being part of something.

'In rehab once, my therapist asked me to draw a picture of myself and my family as I saw them as a child. I drew eight people in a circle holding hands with smiles on their faces – and one little stick person to the side with an unhappy face. That was me. I did not feel part of my family. I didn't feel part of life, society or anything. I felt isolated and alone. That is what drives you to seek connectivity and succour through drugs. It is the sense of wanting to be connected to society and connected to other people.'

Stephen is now a consultant and trainer for drug and alcohol treatment services, helping to bring families back together. He would like to open a rehabilitation centre based on Buddhist principles and perhaps set up a consultancy firm for health providers who want to integrate spirituality into what they are able to offer. He has made a formal commitment to that religion. Buddhism has been a thread through my life, he said.

'You need to love yourself, be at peace with yourself. Finding peace within yourself is an absolute priority.

'When I see an addict now in the street, I know he is only one or two steps from where I am. I remember sitting there in the centre of town, utterly broken. I would see people walking past me, people busy with their lives with their briefcases and suits. That seemed a million miles from me, I used to ache for it. How I wanted that so badly and I've got that now. You are never that far away from it. If you see an addict in the street, you don't have to give them money but look them in the eyes and acknowledge them. Ask them how they are. Moments like that can be profoundly spiritual. I remember times when I have been broken and someone has just looked at me, not ignored me. That actually is very powerful because you are drawn into someone else's reality and you feed off that.

'At the core of us are the same sort of needs for peace, affirmation self-love and self-fulfilment – and the need to be loved and to love.'

THE POWER OF WEAKNESS

On 12 July 2010, close to the battlefields of the First World War, the Trappist monk, Fr Andre Louf, died in his monastery of Mont-des-Cats, France. He was just 34 when he was elected abbot, a ministry he carried out for 34 years, forming generations of monks, some of whom became abbots of other monasteries. He left the office of abbot in 1997 to live as a hermit near a community of Benedictine sisters in Provence. Nourished by the fathers of East and West, he wrote a number of books including *Tuning in to Grace*.[10]

In St Paul's second letter to the Corinthians, we read about the vulnerability of love: 'My grace is sufficient for you, for my power is made perfect in weakness' (2 Cor. 12:9). Grace is simplicity itself, says André Louf, but life in the Holy Spirit is not easy to discern. Different power lines continually cross each other. It is not always apparent how to tell them apart so confusion – or even illusion – remains a possibility, something I have frequently discovered on my vocational trail. Sin, repentance and grace cannot be simply divided into three neat stages because in our everyday experience they are inextricably bound up. They grow together and interact.

In the prologue to his rule, St Benedict says that every day God looks expectantly towards his servant and the time he still measures

ADDICTION AND GRACE

out to us is *ad inducias*, a respite, an extra allowance, a time of grace we receive into the bargain, a period we may use to meet God on another occasion in his marvellous mercy. So every day God works with us, calling us to repentance. As the psalmist puts it, 'Oh that today you would hear his voice: "Harden not your hearts …"'

Is it possible, asks André Louf, for humans to be continually tested, to be continually a miracle of God's grace? The gospels show us in many ways that our advances on this road rarely proceed in a straight line or without obstacles. St Paul, in his Letter to the Corinthians, makes the point about Jesus: 'For he was crucified in weakness, but lives by the power of God.' Christ died on account of human weakness, weakness he had taken upon himself to the ultimate degree; but from that position of vulnerability he arose and now lives by the power of God. In this weakness, which is our weakness, he encountered God's power, and from it he was raised to new life. It is inescapable, says Louf, for any disciple of Jesus, one who wants to walk the road Jesus walked, in turn to stand in his own weakness and therefore temptation.

Jesus came not for the righteous but for sinners, and here, says Louf, we reveal an essential part of Christian experience – perhaps the most important condition for being touched by grace or for being able to tune in on the wavelength of grace. Grace does not connect with our strength or our virtue, but only with our weakness. Accordingly, it is amply sufficient; and therefore we are only strong enough when our weakness has been demonstrated with perfect clarity. For it is precisely the place where the surprise of the grace of Jesus comes from.

TURNING FROM THE LIGHT

One Saturday night I arranged to meet a 33-year-old South African working as a software analyst at the University of Cambridge. David had been introduced to me by a priest in Cape Town. The conversation

WATERSHED

we shared over a meal near Broadcasting House in London was animated. But, as David observed, it also seemed to have a confessional dimension. Even though we were strangers, the 'surprise of grace' was evident.

David's first major 'turning away' from religion happened when he was about 11. He still remembers walking along a brick pathway near his school's prim and proper Methodist chapel almost hidden in the middle of a copse of pine trees. He had just heard another sermon about love, given by Archbishop Desmond Tutu who used to bustle into the small chapel once a week and say things David had never heard from the lips of any other priest – or adult. 'On this occasion, Tutu spoke about God and how caring he was,' David told me. 'But I decided that God did a lot of nothing most of the time and hardly ever responded to prayers. I used to imagine God as a light and I remember turning away from it, like an annoyed lover might turn their face away from a kiss. Yet the pine trees didn't vanish, the smell of their sap remained in the air and natural sunlight still slipped between them, onto the path before me. But I would shut myself away from something beautiful like that and it would be decades before I had the courage to seek it out again.'

Freedom came to South Africa in 1994 and the following year David earned his own after graduating from high school. He believed his time there had somehow inhibited him and that he had suffered the indignities of the education system for far too long. So he explored new freedoms in heavy-drinking weekends. 'I considered myself a Casanova,' he said. 'My friends and I kept score of our conquests. And if I wasn't in the lead, I'd fix the figures. Nothing was ever enough for me. I always wanted more. I believed that the more I threw into life, the more I would get out of it. All my attention was focused on working weeks and partying weekends. I had been smoking a little weed since high school. "What's this?" my brother-in-law once asked, opening the glovebox in my jalopy and spotting a packet. He sniffed it and even looked approvingly, but that was the last he said of it.'

David started dating seriously and says he had some wonderful people in his life but, one by one, found reasons to release them from their services. Some reminded him of the light he had walked away from that day after chapel, but none could simulate it. Their offerings did not fulfil him. He admits that he did begin to wonder why he turned away from the good things in life so often. But he could not find an answer. Then, one day, when he was in his mid-twenties, he fell asleep in the software department where he worked. 'That wouldn't have been so bad,' he recalled, 'except that I was at a staff meeting and woke up with my head on the table – and the rest of the company looking at me. Someone had earlier complained of a smell of booze. I got my first warning at work, which eventually led to my first job loss.

'As the addictions took hold, I began moving from job to job, staying ahead of the warning letters as best I could and leaving before anyone had the chance to let me go. I tried to quit the drugs I'd started, but nothing else in my life had come close to the wonderful oblivion they offered: the warmth of dancing people on a Saturday night, the bright moon at twilight while stoned on the beach, lover after lover, moving from one group of friends to the next, seeking something ever brighter, ever better. I had tried with all my strength to stay clean and sober but nothing had worked. I couldn't understand how I kept on using substances after promising myself I wouldn't. Once, in my early thirties, I crashed my beautiful silver BMW, my pride. Losing it showed me how unmanageable my life had become. It's somehow easier to comprehend the loss of physical objects over spiritual or emotional loss. Losing something material sometimes helped me realise that I was lost spiritually.

'I had nowhere to live. So I found myself surviving on the generosity of friends, in their Wendy house on a parched plot of land in rural South Africa. I ate spinach and coriander grown in their garden, as they were not wealthy either and I had become a burden.

'Occasionally I flirted with death, the death of hope, trust and faith. I also found myself mingling with crooks and gangsters who had an air of violence about them. At one stage I thought that death was preferable to life. I even attempted suicide, I hate to say, using a Stanley knife I found in a drawer. I didn't die then because God had other plans for me – the great flirt, the champion drinker, the fearful mess, the awful failure, which had brought all the pain on myself. I recalled that day at school under the pines and it was as if no time had passed. In many ways I was still that young boy because I think I had stopped growing the moment I had wilfully turned my face away from the light. I'd been existing on borrowed time. I hadn't matured a day spiritually, but my body had grown older, my emotions had been battered and my sanity had gone.

'I admitted this fact to God. I conceded that life had been a dismal place since I had left him. I asked with all the willingness at my command (which was a great deal) to be of service to others, not to be selfish, to live with a clean conscience and to have a working relationship with my higher power. I can still feel the moment my spirituality came back – peace and serenity barrelled into me like a wave that washed all of me away, to be replaced by something new and shiny – the person that God had been waiting for me to become. I haven't touched a drink or drug since. I work my recovery like a cart-horse, along with other like-minded people. We help each other stay clean. I now "turn towards", rather than "turn away". One of my new friends used to work for Desmond Tutu and Nelson Mandela. I consider it no minor detail that God placed him in my life. Although I am not a member of any church, I believe I'm alive today so that I can be in conscious contact with God, living in his name and keeping his principles near to me. In return, he heaps miracles on me.'

Just 18 months after diligently trying to turn his life around, David found himself settled in Britain, walking proudly outside his

ADDICTION AND GRACE

new place of work in Cambridge and into the spring sunshine. He even sent me a text that day expressing his sense of exhilaration. He was on a different continent, so the trees were different, but that didn't matter. The half-starved, wild man from South Africa, who had once feared falling ill to scurvy, had somehow ended up being employed by one of the world's most prestigious seats of learning. It was not what had originally been in his mind but 'my plans paled in comparison to what God could do'. The university wants him to stay on and he's keen to study too.

David admits that he feels his 11-year-old self walking beside him all the time now. 'He's pretty amazed at all the stuff I've been doing. I am too,' he smiled. 'Tutu's message of peace was true and, like so many other people from my country and time, all I had to do was ask God for it. When I wake up every morning my normal response is one of self-interest and self-obsession, not in any malignant sense, but because I'm human. I have to perform acts each day to counteract that, such as entering into prayer or hugging someone drunk who's a storm of elbows and tears. Most of the time, though, it's a thought – and one of gratitude.'

It was evident that Stephen and David were both articulate and engaging conversationalists whose former experiences in different parts of the globe were at times hard to believe. Their stories bore similar traits, and both young men had been brought to their senses in one watershed moment when grace seemed to break through the addiction and cast light on the hard and necessary road to recovery. As the Cistercian monk Thomas Keating has observed, 'To feel one's life unmanageable is itself an experience of the divine.'

In neither situation was there an instant solution, more a searing recognition of their utter impoverishment. Yet from that turning point emerged a desire to reconnect with the spiritual and a resolve to change.

Liberated from the idolatries of our attachments, we discover the freedom and responsibility of love – and to love.

CHAPTER FOUR
STABILITY AND CHANGE

The editorial offices, with their old-fashioned typewriters and creaking floorboards, were straight from the pages of Monica Dickens' satire on provincial journalism, My Turn to Make the Tea. Those of us working late on a Wednesday night would be nourished by slices of Battenburg cake lovingly provided by one of the sub-editors. Hot metal was a production process, not a musical genre. The machines clunked away in the distance. Proof-readers with pince-nez beavered away in two little green offices the size of kiosks. The tiny interview room was also used by the cleaner. When you ushered in a local dignitary for a serious grilling, it was not unusual to discover a mop and bucket on the floor, a dirty rag on the table and a can of spray polish on the chair – if it was still there.

The newspaper, which was meticulously edited, was held in such esteem by the community that it was often referred to as reverentially as one might a holy book. It was a document of record, a gospel of veracity. Getting one's name in print for the right reasons was invariably the subject of local pride. When the flower show tent burnt down one year, an angry reader came into reception (or front counter as we called it) and demanded to know why I had given so much space to the blaze and, in the circumstances, none to his wife's handicraft's stall. 'This has never happened in the history of this newspaper,' he fumed. 'My wife is distraught. She is mentioned *every* year.'

Although my feet became itchy from time to time, they stayed

STABILITY AND CHANGE

under the desk. I didn't really want to move. There was a *stabilitas* about the life that was formative. The staff hardly changed and, in one sense, I don't think I was ever happier. When I wasn't working late, I tore across town in my yellow mini to say evening prayer in my parish church. As Thornton Wilder shows in his 1930s play, *Our Town*, many characters make up a local community and many of them made their way into my column.

These stories were often related to suffering, such as the morning I paced hospital wards talking to survivors of a train fire which had resulted in loss of life and severe injury. One passenger, bandaged from head to toe, revealed to me that the doors of the intercity express had been locked so passengers could not get out. That fact became pivotal to the subsequent inquiry. On another occasion I listened to a woman who told me how she had been scarred by her years in concentration camps decades earlier. She described how a number of her friends had tried to escape Ravensbrück but had been electrocuted on the perimeter fence. The bodies, she said, had been fastened to a Christmas tree around which the other prisoners had been forced to sing carols.

SHOCK, HORROR, CONVERSION

Away from the provinces, I went in pursuit of national stories, especially those with a religious angle. One of them concerned a Christian convert of a most unusual kind – he had formerly worked for the kingdom of Fleet Street. Even then, some of Terry Lovell's colleagues were so sceptical of his new inclinations (so removed were they from the old) that they thought it must be a ruse to get the inside story on Terry Waite who was being held captive in the Lebanon at the time. Another reporter suggested it was a ploy to get redundancy.

'I resigned because of my commitment to Christ. But the years between becoming a Christian and resigning were ones of enormous conflict,' Terry Lovell told me with considerable sincerity one cold February day in Manchester. 'During that three-year period, there were a number of investigations which were very typically Sunday newspaper material. As I grew in my relationship with Christ, each story became much more difficult and seemed much more sordid. The conflict became overwhelming. I was working on three different front-page treatments. On each and every occasion I would go out on these jobs and pray to God to put me in a situation hopefully where I wouldn't have to deceive or to lie or to con people. That's basically what the gutter-press is about. I would go off with Christian music on my car radio and go into church on Sunday, but then go back into the office doing exactly the same thing. As I came to understand and know more of Jesus it became increasingly impossible to continue to do that.'

Long before phone-hacking was making daily news, Terry Lovell said he was repentant about his journalistic proclivities, such as exposing a politician for improper liaisons. 'I felt very sorry for those whose names were emblazoned across the front page or centre-page spread,' he said. 'When reporters move into people's lives, those lives, I believe, are never quite the same again. The public at large are really seen as a playing field for the media, particularly the tabloid press. Lives are destroyed. Relationships are disrupted and destabilised. But for a reporter it's simply another story, another byline, another good week for expenses so I certainly sought God's forgiveness for the harm and hurt that I had caused.

'I know that what I did and the way I did it, many things that way were very wrong with the wisdom of knowing Jesus Christ and knowing his grace. When I look back on those days I can't justify in any way what I did other than to say it was the way of paying the mortgage, which of course is no justification whatsoever.

'To follow Christ and his teachings, and to do one's job successfully as a gutter-press or tabloid reporter is I believe impossible.

STABILITY AND CHANGE

What one is asked to do as a reporter is so frequently at complete odds with one's life as a Christian committed to Jesus. They are mutually exclusive. I couldn't reconcile them and the more I got to know Jesus Christ the more impossible that reconciliation could become or appear. I think society is paying an awful price for the sensational indulgences of the tabloid press.'

These prophetic words of Terry Lovell sprang to mind as I watched Rupert Murdoch and his son James being grilled by MPs during the summer of 2011. But it was Lovell's own 'inside story' which really deserved a banner headline, a conversion of the heart resulting in ownership of the fact that he had been paid to destabilise the lives of others. The change only occurred after he felt unable to continue with his dubious working practices at the same time as embracing his new-found faith. Authentic spiritual transformation cannot be compartmentalised. It affects the whole of who we are, emptying us out so we can be filled again.

WAR AND PEACE

It is not uncommon these days to discover people converting from one faith to another. But, as I travelled through the English country lanes north of London one August afternoon, I was not expecting to meet a young man who had not only switched religions, but countries – and clothes.

'I can connect this tattoo to my spiritual life,' said Vaikuntha Krishna Dass as we chatted in the heart of the Hertfordshire countryside. It was hard to believe that the gentle Hindu monk, sitting beside me in his saffron robes, had been a soldier at the start of the Balkan crisis between 1988 and 1989. Now he was wearing necklaces made from *tulsi*, a common plant in India which protected him from 'anything malicious'. His head was shaven, except for a curl known as a *sika*, a symbol of the fact that, while he had turned his back on bad habits, he had not renounced God.

WATERSHED

The tattoo was the only clue to his past. It had been inscribed on his left arm during military service at a time of unrest between the army and the people of Kosovo. He had been bored one day when he was up in the hills with a Hungarian soldier who had been a tattooist. He had fallen for a girl, ten minutes before he had left for military training. Her name, Maya, along with two hearts, formed the tattoo. But then a letter disclosed that she could wait no longer and had found somebody else. So the tattoo had to be covered with a palm tree. When Vaikuntha joined the Hare Krishna movement, he learned that 'maya' was sanskrit for illusion so the tattoo took on a spiritual significance and a reminder that the romance had been illusory.

By then the soldier had left his native Slovenia for a more peaceful life in England, substituting the Roman Catholic faith of his origins for the wisdom of the East. It was a cultural and religious watershed which was to take Vaikuntha Krishna Dass towards a more rounded understanding of spiritual wholeness.

His day begins at 3.30 every morning when he takes a bath and goes immediately to a room for prayer, meditation, chanting and a lesson from holy scripture. 'Contemplation is the most important factor in my spiritual life,' he told me. 'Without contemplating on the focus and goal of my life, the spiritual would mean mainly an external service. At one point we need to come from the external to an internal devotional practice in service to our Lord. God is everywhere. Contemplating on the Lord in my heart is most uplifting for me. I feel love, protection, shelter, guidance, faith, compassion and humility. Without this focus, life could be dry and mechanical. If we contemplate on material things as a sensual enjoyment and, at the same time, try to contemplate on spiritual things, it is like pouring petrol on the fire. We will never be able to think of God. Our heart will remain hard and we will remain stiff-necked. We cannot follow two masters.'

STABILITY AND CHANGE

Born in Slovenia, Vaikuntha grew up as Vojko Ogrin, a receptive child attuned to the gifts of nature. Having completed compulsory army training in Kosovo, Vojko went on to serve in the police academy. At the time, Slovenia was receiving its independence from Yugoslavia and, detecting imminent clashes, the police were eager to recruit him. 'When I got back from the Army, there were three days to go before we separated ourselves from Yugoslavia. The police were naturally expecting some trouble so they came to my house and invited me to join them. Next day I was supposed to report to the police station around 5 am. They told me to wait for them at the side of the road and they would take me to the police station for training over the next two months. My father's house was in the countryside but, when I opened the door to leave, there was no sound of birds as there had usually been. In fact, there was no sound at all. There was complete silence. That was the beginning of the war. Everything closed down. I walked with my gun to be picked up but nobody came. All I saw was this broken-down tank and some boys looking scared of me as they climbed out of it.

'I was losing something again – this time my freedom. I had an attachment to my country and to my place. I wondered why the peace had been taken away overnight, why people could come and destroy the country. I just wanted to ask people why. But they could not answer.'

Six months later, Vojko noticed a woman going from door to door selling copies of one of the holiest books in the Hindu canon, *The Bhagavad Gita*. As he started to read it himself, something connected. All the questions he had been wrestling with were being answered one by one as he leafed the pages. Surprisingly, he found himself assenting to the philosophy but in neither a sentimental nor fanatical way. His mother was somewhat taken aback to see her son reading an 800-page tome every day. He never perused books, only newspapers. Intrigued to meet the Hare Krishna devotees who had

WATERSHED

been distributing the text, he arranged to go to the local temple. He remembered how impressed he had been with a 'Hare Krishna Experience' he had once watched on television, especially the way in which the monks and nuns were prepared to answer challenging questions. But then he started to hesitate about visiting the temple. The community offered to collect him from his home on several occasions but he made excuses each time. He was too scared and too shy. In the end he relented.

'Inside my heart, I was pulled in because of that book,' he explained. 'It helped me understand the experiences of loss. All the questions I had were answered by that book which recounts a war between two armies in India through the exploits of two figures, Arjuna and Krishna. The questions about suffering that Arjuna raises were the same as mine. I connected straight away with Arjuna. There were two big families: a God-conscious family and one that did not have faith in God; they had knowledge of the spiritual life and religion, but a conflict broke out between the brothers and they lost that faith.

'I was asking myself how I could fight and whether I would lose all my family. Perhaps it would be better, I thought, if I went to the forest like an eastern monk. I was looking for something but I didn't know what I was searching for. I wanted money and opulence but I knew I would never obtain them.

'My move was very subtle. I started going to the temple once a week, then twice a week and then every day. My mother would naturally ask why. I told her about the book and said I liked the people. She was fine about it until I said I would be going to Italy to visit another temple. I said I would be away a few weeks but I did not return until three months later, although I was in contact with her. My decision was very difficult for my parents, brothers and sisters to accept especially because, before then, I would never go anywhere and certainly never out of my country. I hadn't left Slovenia until I joined the Hare Krishna movement.'

STABILITY AND CHANGE

Vojko's two-year induction took him to the Florentine countryside in Italy and a more meditative life surrounded by bamboo forest, mountains and cows. He realised he was looking for a 'high-thinking ethos in a simple environment'. The training covered theory and practical experience (such as how to chant the name of God), philosophy, higher education and an introduction to a spiritual teacher to guide him personally.

He was sent to the headquarters of the Hare Krishna Movement in the United Kingdom, Bhaktivedanta Manor in Hertfordshire, a house once owned by the Beatle George Harrison. There, he met his spiritual teacher and, at the age of 21, took part in an initiation into the chanting of the holy name of God (Krishna) which took the form of a fire sacrifice. He promised to obey four principles which included not having any illicit relationship with a woman, only through marriage; not becoming intoxicated through drink or drugs; refraining from eating meat and promising not to gamble. 'Giving up was easy for me because I was a vegetarian before, the only gambling I took part in was playing lottery; I would have one beer in a month and never smoked. And I had never had sexual relations with women. There was nothing to give up.'

Vaikuntha told me that he thought his relationship with his family had improved since he became a monk. It had become less impersonal. Members of his family used to mind each other's business until they had lunch on Sundays. Now they were curious. Some friends and neighbours had been to see him in England and took word back to parents who are not ready to see their son in his monastic habitat, although he does return to Slovenia. 'Even my mother says I have changed for the better. There were certain difficulties in our family life. I wasn't affected by those things. I would have run away and let the family sort it all out. Now we can sit down, talk and try to understand why we are quarrelling. My sister is my best friend now whereas before she was just my sister. When I left

WATERSHED

home, she was 13. Now she is married with one baby. When she was pregnant, she did not want to tell my mother in case she became angry. After an eight-year gap, she contacted me and asked if I could explain the situation to our mum. I am much calmer and more open-minded. I can understand people easier. I feel I am here and available to others. If I can manage this for the rest of my life, this is the most beautiful thing I can achieve.

'I don't feel I have lost anything. But I think I have gained a lot. The former life is still there but there is another life on top of that. The struggles are still there. The temptations remain. But they would be there whether I was a monk or not. I personally accepted them as my struggles and my temptations but, when you have a taste of higher things, they are manageable. They won't affect your life or your health. Everything has to be followed according to the order. Renunciation is actually my struggle but I don't suffer as a result. I embrace those struggles with happiness because I struggled before I joined this movement. Every monk will say he is struggling. There is a sexual desire and a desire for wealth, but monks have been there and they renounce those things with knowledge.'

There had been, he felt, significant changes too in his personality. In Slovenia he had been reserved and kept to himself. He could never have imagined going to the theatre, for example. When he moved into the temple, he discovered there was a theatre group. The manager even asked him to take part in a play. Embarrassed by his accent, he could not imagine performing in front of a sea of faces observing and listening. In the end, he agreed to go on stage but only in a latex mask so he could not be recognised. Later he undertook some dramatic training and realised he had a hidden talent. 'I discovered I could be a performer. Becoming a monk means using your nature and your talents for serving God. If I have a talent of acting, I can act. But let me put a message about God through drama and that's how it becomes spiritual.

STABILITY AND CHANGE

'I think my mind is now more open to the world. I think I am more personable. I see this world with open eyes and am trying to see beyond it. My life is more pure. It is as simple as that. Slovenia was such a small country. You never think of going anywhere. I had never heard of any other religion than Catholicism or met anyone who wasn't from Slovenia. I only spoke Slovenian and didn't know about work.'

Since becoming a monk, Vaikuntha has travelled the world a lot as part of the order's missionary work. He said he did not only want to share spiritual knowledge and philosophical ideas but to care for others and to clothe them. His chief inspiration was a Christian saint – Francis of Assisi. At the time of the tsunami in Sri Lanka, he worked among the Buddhists living in the south of the country. He helped cook vegetarian meals for two thousand people over a three-month period – 'I just wanted to give my time for them coming from a rich organised country. I wanted to go down there. They lost all that beauty. I didn't find people lamenting and running around in despair. They were very hopeful. They had a spark in their eyes and that hope.

'When I arrived they were a bit surprised to find a Hare Krishna monk from the West with robes. I worked in an orphanage with children who had lost parents, brothers and sisters. They were waiting for someone to pick them up and take them home. I was a monk from a community that talks a lot about spirituality, renunciation and not-attachment. In front of me were people who were not asking for those things in their desperate situation. They had lost everything but were still smiling. I felt so sad. I had been told I might not be needed there but I knew I had to go. I had three days to organise myself and collect enough money to buy the air ticket. It was my karma, destiny and duty to go there. I grew up spiritually there. It was as though I had lost my own people. I also travelled to Haiti after the earthquake. Again, I went through Food For Life Global.'

WATERSHED

What was especially surprising to learn was that Vaikuntha Krishna Dass considered himself a better Catholic now because he was a Hindu monk. Furthermore, he had no reservations about going to any Catholic church or monastery and talking with any Christian monk about Jesus, St Francis, Krishna or the prophet Muhammad. He said he now practised what he preached. In his Slovenian days he would say he used to say he was a Catholic but couldn't show people his Catholic life. Now he was able to reveal his spirituality as a way of life rather than merely a label. He lived that life and had become that life. He felt his earlier anxieties about loss had been subsumed into his Hindu identity, even replaced by it.

'After becoming a Hindu monk, I was introduced to an amazing devotional lifestyle and spiritual knowledge about the soul, creation, God, our relationship with God and our real identity. For me an eye was opening, not only about God but also about religions in general. I knew that everything was in the heart but I also realised I needed the guidance and shelter of an institution.'

Yet, as the years have gone by, he has found himself reconnecting with the Catholic spiritual tradition. A friend gave him a statue of Mary and a set of rosary beads with which he now prays every day. From that moment, something significant happened. 'I felt Mary's warm presence in my heart. I wanted to know more about her and Jesus. I started reading the biographies of different Catholic saints like Francis, Anthony, Thérèse of Lisieux, Teresa of Avila, Bernadette of Lourdes and Padre Pio. I get so much inspiration from them, even though I am still a monk in the Hare Krishna temple. I will take to heart anyone who can bring me closer to God.'

JUSTICE AND MERCY

Listening to Vaikuntha it was apparent that a change of direction was not the same as a conversion, while stability did not mean a curtailment of liberty. But, on the other hand, a restriction of freedom

STABILITY AND CHANGE

can lead to a conversion. For the past six months I have been corresponding with a prisoner in the United States. Edward, who is 32, is now out on parole so we keep in touch via email. But his long letters from behind bars, immaculately written on yellow paper, revealed to me a man of authentic prayer who had not only paid the price for his misdemeanours but had also come to deep faith during his time inside. Accountability for him had resulted not in resentment or retaliation but in a religious conversion and a new-found commitment as a Catholic educator, teaching other inmates the principles of faith.

During our exchanges, we discussed politics, religion, ethics and spirituality, and we shared opinions on Julian of Norwich, Thomas Merton and St Francis of Assisi. Edward told me how he loved to pray the Magnificat. In turn I learnt much about prison life and its unique language. I followed him through the endless routines of every day, as he woke at 6.15, worked in the library, walked in the yard and returned to his cell for the regular counts to make sure no one had escaped. He told me about his fellow inmates and the psychological games that some staff played with them.

Edward wasn't afraid to share his own vulnerability. His faith didn't protect him from difficulties, crises or betrayals, he said, but enabled him to look at his past with responsibility and the future with hope. He said that it was difficult to follow all the church's teachings and, like all of us, he fell along the way. But what brought him to his feet again was a belief in 'the infinite mercy of God and the saving power of Jesus'. Through a disciplined spiritual practice within those walls, he had grown daily into a deeper, personal relationship with God.

Being uprooted from our familiar trappings or comfortable lifestyles is never easy and feelings of displacement can soon swamp us. But, as the conversations with Terry, Vaikuntha and Edward seem to prove, there can be no real growth without an openness to change

WATERSHED

or to be changed. As the Irish spiritual writer Sister Stan puts it, 'Every little death we die, every little letting go, turns us into something new.'

This was something I held on to as I reflected on my own change of direction. Although long ago I had discerned a distinct calling to work in the world of the media – a Benedictine monk once assured me it was an apostolate – there came a point when I began to feel compromised and sensed that something else was being asked of me. For the itinerant journalist, the move would lead me into greater stability not away from it.

CHAPTER FIVE
HURT AND HEALING

Many of us have been hurt at some time or another by the comments and actions of other people – as well as by institutions. Hurts can trigger a watershed in view of their capacity to change relationships and lead us to a radical reassessment of our very selves. Sometimes these wounds go back to childhood or adolescence. They may be caused by people who secretly envy or resent us. Even years of therapy or spiritual direction may not completely eradicate the psychological pain which can resurface unexpectedly.

Being vulnerable to criticism ourselves does not always immune us from injuring the feelings of others. We might harbour resentment for something someone (or some institution) said or did to us in the past without any self-realisation that something we said or did to someone else caused them hurt and offence at the time. Hurts, then, are not always intentional. What appear to us to be careful and reasonable words might be received as offensive and insensitive. It is always difficult to know how our remarks will be interpreted or absorbed. Sometimes we learn only of their impact years later.

The truth about ourselves is often the hardest to hear and we may protect ourselves from the reality by claiming (sometimes dramatically) that we have been hurt. Both self-absorption and emotional manipulation may be at work in the complex world of hurt. But there are pastoral approaches which seek to heal.

'A sensitive sharing with someone at a carefully chosen moment reassures the person that the words come from a good intention,'

WATERSHED

says British counsellor Tim Pike. 'The person is respected as they are but have a choice as to whether or not to act on the shared observation.'

If someone is hurt by the words of another, a healthy detachment is sometimes advisable. This is not denial but an honest acknowledgement of the *feeling* and a realisation that it will lessen in intensity and go in its own time, however slowly. But Tim Pike points out that it's important to understand that our feelings are not the same as our identity. They come and go, and we have the power to watch and observe them rather than *become* them. This easily happens when admitting, for example, that 'I am humiliated'. A new language that says 'humiliation is here right now' provides a more realistic and digestible context that allows the feeling to travel through and move on in its own time. 'This detached approach does not merge our identity with feelings but places them alongside, consciously, acknowledged and accepted,' says Tim Pike. 'We accept the feeling is there first and then move beyond blame and harbouring. But it's about consciously accepting that the wound is there. It is present. We cannot control how long it will remain, but it can teach and direct us while it accompanies our pilgrimage.'

Sometimes those who love us most can hurt us most, according to the pastoral theologian and prolific spiritual writer Henri J. M. Nouwen. The author of *The Wounded Healer* does not suggest ways of how our wounds can be healed easily but points out that the more we open ourselves up to being healed, the more we realise how deep our wounds really are. A search for true healing is always a suffering search. The challenge lies in living the wounds through rather than thinking them through. It is preferable to feel the pain rather than understand it, to allow wounds to enter your silence rather than attempt to talk about them. If you let the hurts move around in your head, then you end up constantly analysing rather than healing them. You need to forget the questions swirling around

HURT AND HEALING

in your mind about why you were hurt and so on. Instead, advises Nouwen, you need to let your wounds go down to your heart and trust its healing power. 'There your hurts can find a safe place to be received, and once they have been received, they lose their power to inflict damage and become fruitful soil for new life.'[11]

Nouwen suggests thinking of each wound as you would of a child who has been hurt by a friend. As long as the child tries to get back at the friend, one wound leads to another. But when the child receives the consolation of a parent, she or he can live through the pain, forgive and build up a new relationship. Nouwen believes people who have been hurt should be gentle with themselves, and let their heart be their embracing parent as the wounds are lived through.

THE COURAGE TO FORGIVE

With its boats in the rectory garden and deer on the driveway, St Peter's Catholic Church, Big Pine Key, Florida, was my kind of place. I liked its mission statement too: 'No matter what your present status in the Catholic Church, no matter what your current family or marital situation, no matter what your past or present religious situation, no matter your personal history, age, background, race, etc., no matter what your own self-image or esteem, you are invited, welcomed, accepted, loved and respected.'

I had been invited to spend a week there and to give a talk on the spirituality of Henri Nouwen. I met parishioners in their elegant homes beside canals and received prodigious hospitality. I went to Mass every day in a side chapel where we were obediently joined by a Labrador called Scratch who pattered in every morning behind the celebrant, sat quietly during the Eucharist, then pattered out again after the blessing with a natural sense of duty and timing. It was there that I became aware that God was undoubtedly calling me to embrace another way of life.

WATERSHED

Among the worshippers was a remarkable woman in her 80s, a gentle and generous person with inner depth and strength. Hilda E. Doody, a retired teacher, felt so close to God that if she happened to miss morning Mass her day seemed incomplete. Living in a cottage beside one of the waterways, she still dived for lobsters. Born in Puerto Rico to a farming family, close to the sea, she learned to love nature from a young age and began a lifelong fascination with calves which she observed from her bedroom window. Her family taught the Catholic faith to farm workers who were encouraged to pray before lunch. There was no doubt in Hilda's mind that her own vocation lay in teaching. 'My first students were the butterflies which I loved very much,' she said. 'I didn't realise at the time that you're not supposed to disturb them. I still love butterflies.' Butterflies, of course, are symbols of resurrection as well as healing.

Hilda's first teaching assignment, by choice, was at a school situated on a mountain where her family owned another farm managed by 'a wonderful caretaker'. She rode a horse from where the public bus dropped her to the two-room school. This was a way for Hilda to repay 'these wonderful people for all the work they did'.

During her last two years in secondary school, Hilda convinced her family to allow her to change from an all-girls' private Catholic school to a co-ed private school. It wasn't easy, but she won. It was at this new school that she discovered her prowess as an all-round athlete. At the age of 17, she was part of a team which represented Puerto Rico in the 1944 Caribbean Olympics at Barranquilla, Colombia. She excelled at several events including the broad jump, javelin throwing, the 50-yard dash and the obstacles.

But it was a much more recent ordeal that proved to be a watershed for Hilda in terms of her own dependence on God, and her retelling of it taught me much about the power of faith and forgiveness. It was hard to believe that, at the age of 76, Hilda had

HURT AND HEALING

become the victim of an attempted strangulation and suffocation in her own home, left for dead by someone she knew and loved, an intelligent, caring person whose mind went out of control.

'It happened in my own home in darkness,' she explained. 'It began one evening at 7.10 and I was still lying there in the dark at 9.30. In my desperation, I implored the Holy Spirit which I had been taught to do since I was very young: "What do I do? I know I can't hear you but tell me." The prayer saved me from the strangulation. I was supposed to die at that moment. My concerns were about what to do with my neck and what to do with my body. I hadn't read about how to defend myself, but I asked the Holy Spirit to guide me. I was left for dead, lying at the last place I was thrown. I just kept on praying and asking the Holy Spirit to tell me what to do. I stretched myself because I couldn't breathe well. I had pillows put over me to stop me from breathing. I found the air passages in there but I didn't move. That's when the person probably thought I was dead.'

Even in the pain and distress of that situation, Hilda found herself naturally identifying with the sufferings of Christ. 'I said to him, "I know that you suffer for me and I'm suffering but I still have things to do in this world so guide me so I can complete my cycle in this world." It was completely dark and I said, "I must escape from this house. Help me Holy Spirit." Much as I hurt, I got up from that bed, picked up a bag, which I always keep with extra things in case of an emergency, went through the back to the garage, got in the car and said to the Holy Spirit, "Take me where I am supposed to go."'

Hilda ended up in the church dining hall, to which she had keys. She rang the priest who immediately called for an ambulance, though Hilda was reluctant for him to contact the police. At the hospital, medics X-rayed her neck, then treated and bandaged the many bodily lacerations that had been caused by the attack. Hilda told the police to delay their arrest: 'I said to them, "Don't do anything. Let that person sleep. That person was in a semi-state and had lost his mind. It was not malicious."'

'I still live in the same place where the attack happened. I think of it but it does not scare me. Attending Mass every day helps me. I grew through the experience but you have to forgive – forgive no matter what because the person loves. I had already forgiven the person by the time the police arrived. That's why I said, "Let that person rest."'

Hilda then told me, 'When I heard the voice of Henri Nouwen at your presentation saying "The person who hurts you is the one who loves you most" I could relate to that right away.'

The capacity to forgive is an essential ingredient in the healing of hurt.

ESCAPE AND SANCTUARY

An actor, said Bernard Miles, founder of the Mermaid Theatre in London, scatters blessings and passes the benediction on. He is a member of the healing fraternity. For even at its worst the stage is 'a solace, a cure for loneliness, a gathering together in the name of mankind'.[12]

Film actor and producer Craig Conway knows exactly what Lord Miles meant. Craig grew up on a tough council housing estate in Tyne and Wear where he suffered at the hands of an alcoholic father. A warm, intelligent, earthy Geordie, Craig embraced the theatre as a place of psychological and spiritual transfiguration, an arena of grace. For him, it became a sanctuary and refuge.

When we met at a flamboyant London restaurant, designed as an opera house, close to the theatres of Covent Garden, Craig told me how his childhood had been shaped by the dual combination of passion and aggression. His mother was an open-hearted, artistic woman with a love of oil painting, literature and food. 'I had these really beautiful moments where my mother taught me how to paint if

HURT AND HEALING

I was frightened,' Craig said. 'If there was a thunderstorm, she would sit and draw with me to get me over that.' But as a result of his drinking, Craig's father – a butcher by day and a 'mad performer and singer' by night – was prone to bouts of extreme violence which overshadowed an otherwise creative upbringing. The situations the boy encountered in the home resulted in frequent nightmares which persisted into adolescence.

Craig ended up living with his sister, although his brother, who had a different father, was not allowed to stay with him – he had to reside with their grandmother. 'My father didn't like my brother in the house because he reminded him that my mother had had another man,' Craig explained over a bottle of Pinot Grigio. 'This created a burden of anxiety for him so, when he got drunk, all that came out and caused the violence to spill over. A lot of it came in the form of shouting and abuse, grabbing and being flung around. Once my mother held me in her arms while my father was beating her. I can still trace the smell of fear coming from my mother while this was happening. It was unbelievable, yet also very theatrical at the same time.

'If there had been a quiet few days, I would come home from school scared in case something was about to happen. One day, when I was about six, I heard my mother screaming in the house after she had opened the door to my father. She had a towel to her face. The towel went from being a pale white to an instant red. He had broken her jaw. Mum said, "Run, run, to your Auntie Joyce's," a friend of hers. I just remember racing up the road, screaming my eyes out. I knew I had to keep running.

'Shortly afterwards, we left our father. For a couple of years, he had custody of his children for a weekend and he would come to the house. One time he arrived with a shotgun. He had been keeping us out later and later. Our solicitors told us that, if we intended to end the custody, then we had to tell him to his face that we did not want to see him again. That's what I had to do that weekend, standing by the back door.'

With an innate sense of the theatrical, Craig managed to recognise the comic-tragic dimensions of the domestic drama and somehow, throughout it all, found himself becoming 'someone who was afraid of the world but someone who also had a place in it'. They were times of both security and insecurity. In a chilling pattern of predictability, the children ascertained that in order for them to feel close and loved, and have a sense of belonging, something tragic had to happen. There was either an overload of love and security, or periods of pain, upset and fear. Craig carried that complexity into his adolescence, yet at the same time discerned the formation of an inner confidence. He knew he wanted to connect with people and have fun. He had always been the clown in the class. But his family experiences had led to severe bullying by school kids and peer groups who noticed how close he had grown to his mother.

'I was always the bully's friend but also his greatest enemy which was bizarre,' Craig explained. 'I was putting myself in situations and associating with people who were quite tragic characters. I had a lot of compassion because I wanted the world to become a better place. I suppose every naive child has dreams like that. So I would find myself mixing with the bullies in order to help them. I'd had a hard time and I wanted to be there for them. I would push it to the extent where I would frustrate them and, of course, when we reached the point where we knew we were too young to handle what was going on, it would turn into violence. I felt I understood the mind of the bully because I always felt compassion for my father, even though at times I hated what he did and could not understand why he would do it.'

As the years went by, there was only one place where Craig felt safe – the stage. The discovery proved a watershed for him. As

HURT AND HEALING

soon as he walked into any area of creativity or stepped into a room where there was an easel, board and some paints, Craig sensed security because he was in touch with his emotions and could control his expression of them. When he took part in his first school performance, he suddenly noticed hundreds of people looking at him, eager to hear what he had to say. He felt he was bringing them pleasure. Furthermore, watching an audience laughing or crying at his performances convinced him of his own self-worth. After his experience of domestic disintegration, this was salvation for him.

Craig joined a 'devising theatre' and other groups in the North East, spending time among like-minded people with whom he could discuss his problems. When fear or panic gripped him at home, he knew he would be able to find a theatrical setting where he could use characters and role-play to explore the inner fears. He learned to accept the emotions as feelings that could not destroy him. Through plays, he could even express and explore violence without any bodily contact. Life on the stage evolved naturally into 'an absolutely safe haven'.

He left school at 15 with a B+ in GCSE painting and drawing, a D in drama – 'because I never did the written work' – and a pass in English. Increasingly drawn to a full-time career in the theatre, Craig gained experience in local drama groups and badgered directors for small roles in visiting productions. He took part in community theatre plays in schools and colleges, living on people's floors and believing that persistence would be enough to see him through.

But Craig also knew that, in order to become his true self and fulfil his potential, he would have to leave the area of Britain he loved. It would be personally and socially challenging to break out of the North East, a place of beauty, compassion and, sometimes, volatile honesty, but also a region rooted in the remembrance of its self. Geordies, I was told, like people to know they are the

WATERSHED

northerners. They never forget their origins. Although this protective outlook on life had been a grounding for Craig, he realised it could stand in the way of his achieving the goals he had set his heart on. In that way, he admitted, the environment of the North East could have a destructive streak. 'If you leave your street, it's tragic. All your friends say, "Why are you leavin' us? Think you're better than us?"' If he had stayed in the Newcastle area, he reckons he would now be either in prison or dead. 'I got into a lot of drug-taking, lived as the typical young male sleeping around and getting involved with a lot of mixed-up and confused people who were connected to local gang warfare,' he confessed. 'My first relationship was with a 24-year-old woman with two kids. She came from a battered wives' home. Her ex-boyfriend once came back to the town and said to me, "Why are you here? Look around you. Look at the state of what we are. You've so much more to offer. Go and do your acting." All of that contributed to the fact that I had a real compassion for people who went through pain. I wanted to know their stories. I wanted to fight for their injustices.'

At the age of 19, Craig Conway was offered his first television role in the BBC's *Our Friends in the North*, working alongside Christopher Ecclestone and Daniel Craig. This led to roles ranging from a characterisation of George Orwell in a stage production of *Homage to Catalonia* to Scar the Beast in a Pinewood horror movie, *The Descent*. His work has since taken him to Spain, France, Russia and Canada. He also gained a reputation in physical theatre, renowned for his one-man show playing an aggressive, violent bouncer in Jeff Thomson's *Doorman*. 'The body is an expressive tool and, before you speak, the body has to be engaged. You don't need sets. You just need to turn up and be the space. I think I owe a lot of my life in the theatre, television or film to my upbringing.

'I think what my childhood did offer me was a sense of harsh reality. The world is a hard place, no matter how wonderful you want

HURT AND HEALING

it to be. No matter what stage you are at, you will face difficulty. This is what allows me to be grounded. I don't think I will ever lose grip of who or what I am. But it doesn't make me a better actor or entitle me to discuss things because of that. Many people have had many wonderful stable upbringings and will have just as much, if not, at times, more passion than I could have.'

Violence and beauty can co-exist in the theatre, he believes. People cannot ignore the fact that theatre can be 'violently beautiful'. There is always a violence to something beautiful, always something joyful about tragedy. This came to light when he made a documentary drama with young offenders and when he wrote *Car Trouble*, a play about growing up as a young man in Manchester. Produced at the city's Contact Theatre, it brought together 15 young Mancunians. It was 'a violent and beautiful' piece of work, written in verse and opening many doors for young actors or those interested in the theatre. Nothing gave him more joy than to see them giving expression positively to their feelings on stage.

Theatre, he intuits, has a spiritual quality in the sense that it is a place where you can express yourself without having to hold back. It also provides a space of vulnerability in which actors can create states of sensitivity for themselves and out of which flows beauty. Even if they never work in the theatre again, young people will realise they have something of worth to accompany them through life.

'Humanity and its survival relies on the fact that we, as human beings, see beyond ourselves and by seeing beyond ourselves we gain a deeper understanding of who we are,' he said. 'Theatre does that in all of its truth. That is why it is a spiritual experience. It has made me a better person. It has allowed me to be angry, fearful, passionate and loving, and to enter worlds I would not otherwise have got to know.'

Whatever the role, Craig said his primary instinct had always been to explore the character's emotive response to a particular situation. At the same time, his own emotional turbulence – 'where the highs have been very high and the lows have been very low' – enabled him to handle the extremes. 'The real me has probably been seen by more people than myself,' he admitted. 'I think the real me comes out through various characters and the roles that I am given. When you play a character that has an emotion, you have to find a connection with it. The only way you find that as an actor is by drawing on your own experience. The character makes you access something in your past or something that is happening to you now so you can bring that out or portray it. It forces you to expose your inner self. That is what you do on stage. You expose yourself. You take yourself to the most vulnerable point you can so the audience can take what they need.

'But it is a vulnerability the actor may not want to enter into in his or her personal life. In my personal life, I am more cautious. The camouflage exists more in my real life than on the stage. If I didn't have the theatrical outlet, I think I would be a very scared person.

'People might come up to me after a show and say that I have really affected them. Part of me wants to reply that it is all a skill or technique. But it is not. It is actually me saying that I am a person with an emotion. I am affected too and the character affects me.'

When he first walked on stage at The National – to work in the ensemble of *Romeo and Juliet* and in *Peer Gynt* for Trevor Nunn – the lad from the Tyne was awestruck. He needed to spend time imbibing the atmosphere on his own. He was witnessing 'a space that had been taken over by various artists that I have loved and admired'.

Craig says that, when he goes into a theatre, he usually says a prayer, virtually asking the theatre, that space, to allow him to speak his mind or express freedom. There is 'almost a reverence' in certain theatres as a result of the historic productions they have housed. For Craig there is even the feeling that he is 'an apostle of this god that

HURT AND HEALING

is theatre'. There is also something eucharistic about performance, he feels. 'I do feel at times very blessed – and that is the word – because the stage has allowed me to live. I mean that in a very full sense. It has not just permitted me to have a good lifestyle. It has actually enabled me to connect. It is almost as though we give these sacrificial offerings. We offer the script, and then the actors come along and break the bread. We turn it into something else and eventually we become these priests who preach it. We are evangelical. We stand there and preach the word of theatre. It is postmodern religion. It is a devotion. And I do not believe anybody can be a part of this world unless they have a lifetime commitment.'

The theatre was also 'the couch to lie on and talk to,' he said. In that way it had been his saviour. But it had also been the place that has educated him and allowed him not only to give what he wanted to the world but to feel part of the bigger picture. Whether performing in regional, national or international productions, there was a relationship with the world at large in blunt contrast to his childhood memories of finding the local environment insular and one he felt alienated from. The theatre had dispelled that confusion and opened up a means of investigating the world. 'When players create the question and the audience start asking it, then art is born. Art at its best makes people question their world. Even now, if I walk into a theatre, I find the idea that this space in front of me can be transformed into anything creates in me a sense of absolute calm and a real passion to want to explore and investigate myself. Whenever you go into a theatre, whether it's full or empty, you start looking inwardly and bringing things out. It gives you a feeling of enlightenment to be in a space and think, "Well, I can transform this."'

There are no limitations in theatre, he explains, and that is what provides the stage with its ultimate safety. Moreover, it is impossible to fail in theatre. Whether a show is good or bad is beside the point. An actor cannot be a failure so long as he or she is 'investigating and exploring theatre'. Whatever is being produced 'in that sacred space' is something new and can never be repeated. 'You can create a great show but you can't necessarily re-create that one moment when it is completed in its entirety for the first time. Although it's the same show the next day, by the following night it will have changed. It will be different and the audience will bring something new to it as well. Together you come away with a shared experience. I do not know any other industry that can create that.'

Once an escape route from a hostile world, the theatre took on the guise of a refuge for Craig where he could hide from the person he was and not feel obliged to admit what had happened to him in the past. But the more he has remained in the theatrical world, the more he has realised that, in order to become more disciplined and informed about his craft, the more he has needed to get in touch with his inner self. 'Eventually you always come back to your self,' he acknowledged. 'It is the Peer Gynt syndrome – you can run around the world, but at the end of the day, the one thing that will make your life worthwhile is your self. Luckily, theatre will always bring you back to who you are as a person, even though it may remain undefined as such. You have to know your self and be able to offer your self in order to create something worthwhile.

'Theatre is always evolving, caught between worlds. When something happens on the planet, theatre changes. At the time of the terrorism attacks on 9/11, people alerted their gaze to the theatres to assess whether their productions were appropriate. Theatres exist purely because of their environment – the world. Theatre provides us with a question and that may want us to provide actions to be the catalyst for a bigger action, a movement of something. Who knows, something may happen in the world one day that theatre will not be able to express.'

Influenced by such theatrical giants as Peter Brook, Joe Orton, Steven Berkoff and Bertolt Brecht, Craig Conway detects within

HURT AND HEALING

theatre what he describes as 'a breath'. Performance is always about something that can change naturally and live, and his sense of spirituality is likewise derived from anything that has breath. 'When I witness somebody in a state of panic, fear or joy, the first thing I always pick up on is somebody's breath,' he said. 'With some people, you can't even feel them breathing or relaxing. I have this real urge to put my hand on somebody's chest and say "Breathe out – I want to hear you breathe." When I write, direct or perform, I try to detect the breath pattern to what I am doing and that seems to produce something that is real. This can go beyond the realms of reality and take me into somewhere heightened and spiritual. I cannot put my finger on what that might be. I can just suggest that it comes from the breath of what I do. It does not include a notion of God but of eternity.

'I think that, in some way, many people have this sense. For me, God is an eternal sense of something. For me, theatre is completely eternal and, by being an actor in that somewhere, I will always be a part of that world. We should encourage people to express themselves positively in a safe environment. I think in some ways we have to be aware of how beautifully complex we all are – and appreciate that fact. I forget sometimes and get very annoyed. But I try my best to find everybody's story and give everybody a worth, I'll trust anybody until proved otherwise. That finds expression in theatre. Some people use drama as therapy. Theatre provides a forum for life's events ands that's a great tool we have.'

It is unquestionably the theatre that has had most paternal influence on Craig Conway. 'The theatre completely became my father,' he said. 'It was my education as a man. I was able to express myself as a man and even more as well. I looked up to a lot of my friends and their fathers. But the one thing I hated was the fact that the men were too masculine, whereas the maleness of theatre is something very beautiful, tender and sensitive. A lot of North East men are not brought up to be that way. I was raised by my mother, grandmother and sister, so I had a very feminine upbringing which I think contributed to the bullying. But theatre had a different kind of masculine image. It was quite big, strong and powerful, yet it also possessed this beautiful sensitivity so it was definitely a father figure to me.'

Craig has become a father himself to Harvey Rhys Halfpenny through his marriage to the actress Jill Halfpenny. Although they have divorced, they remain close friends, devoted to their son. Craig says he now finds himself exploring realms of childhood that were denied him. He believes we can learn from the youngest of minds. Fatherhood has led to a new philosophy of life which offers its own guidance to those wrestling with how to heal their past hurts: 'Go with the ebb and flow of the world around you, keep asking questions, be bold and ambitious, keep on believing in yourself. Let go of your ego and live the heart you are.'

CHAPTER SIX
LOSS AND HOPE

All of us have experienced loss at some time in our lives, whether it be a relative, relationship, job or self-esteem. It is a universal experience and yet affects each of us in different ways. Often the story of another person's loss puts ours into perspective.

When, in March 2011, I learned that Catholic police constable Ronan Kerr had been murdered in an explosion at Omagh, I was reminded of another atrocity carried out there by paramilitaries in Northern Ireland. A previous car bomb attack on Saturday 15 August 1998 by the Real Irish Republican Army (a splinter group of the former Provisional Irish Republican Army whose members opposed the Belfast Agreement) killed 29 people. A further 220 were injured. Many were out shopping with their families and friends. The fatalities included two unborn children. The blast, described by the BBC as Northern Ireland's worst single terrorist atrocity, was so powerful that the bodies of several victims were never found.

Shortly before the inquests, I travelled to Omagh to meet Michael Gallagher whose 21-year-old son Aiden died that day. As I entered the house, Michael showed me a photograph of Aiden taken on his graduation day. 'It is always painful to look at that smiling face – somebody who had such a future and wanted such a future,' he said.

Michael Gallagher, who helped set up the Omagh Support and Self-Help Group, talked quietly about the atrocity. I listened intently as he relived the emotional turmoil of that day. At one level it provided information for my radio report. At another level it was

WATERSHED

preparation for the day when, in a future pastoral role, I might find myself sharing a person's grief in tragic circumstances.

'That Saturday morning was bright and beautiful, one of the few good days of the summer,' Michael Gallagher recalled. 'Aiden had got up early, gone out and returned at lunchtime. I came in and asked my wife where he was. He was upstairs getting changed before going down to the town to buy some jeans and a pair of boots. I'll never forget when he walked down the hall and looked around for what would be the last time. He said, "I'll not be long." 'Aiden left and, a short time after, I went back to the garage and continued working underneath a car. Then I heard a very loud explosion. I knew right away it was a bomb. I got up, walked out of the garage, closed the door, and headed towards Omagh which was two miles away. I could see a plume of smoke rising in the distance but I couldn't tell which part of the town that it was from.

'When I got back home, my wife and daughter, Cathy, were very agitated and worried. We could hear the sirens and the helicopters. We just tried to console each other. We were looking for whatever news we could but we couldn't ring anywhere because the phones weren't working. Cathy switched on the television. In a very short time, it seemed, they were talking about ten people being dead. I asked her to turn off the TV and not to put it on again.

'I decided to go to the county hospital because I believed that, if Aiden had been injured, he would have been taken there. There was no point going to the scene because there would be too many there. So I arrived at the back entrance to the hospital where the casualty department was located. People were arriving in ambulances, private cars and vans. Some were on foot because the hospital was only half- a- mile from the bomb scene. As I walked up to casualty, there seemed to be hundreds of people standing outside with injuries. In the background I could see an army helicopter about to take off and another waiting to land. It just reminded me of a

LOSS AND HOPE

scene from Vietnam, except they weren't soldiers but women and children.

'When I went in through the hospital, I could have gone to any treatment room because there were very few staff on. Some of the sights were quite horrific. I remember seeing in the hallway one woman believed to be dead. I went through all the wards but I couldn't find Aiden. So I went back home again. I lit a candle and put it in the window. The father of Michael Barrett, the friend Aiden had been in town with, arrived. We both went to where we knew Aiden would have parked the car. In the car park, there were just two cars. I knew then that there was something very seriously wrong because, if Aiden had left, he would have already been home – or if he had had access to a telephone he would have called home.

'We went back to the hospital but again we couldn't find Aiden. We went home, then returned a third time when we discovered Michael Barrett in one of the wards. He was very badly burned. I asked him where Aiden was. He said he had been beside him when the bomb exploded but he didn't know where he was now. We left and were told to go to the leisure centre where all the information was being collated.

'We spent about the next 14 hours there. Then, in the early hours of the morning, we were asked down to a side room. There was a policeman, a policewoman and a social worker. We just knew by the nature of the questions that we weren't going to have the outcome that we wanted. Later that morning, we were taken to an army camp where we were told there was someone fitting Aiden's description in the temporary mortuary. One of the helicopter hangers had been transformed. The army went to great trouble to make sure that it was as pleasant as that sort of place could be. It was dignified and we were very grateful for that. But it was very difficult.

'After that, I had to go back and tell my wife and two daughters the bad news. That was very, very painful. When I went into the hall, they were there. All I could say was that Aiden wouldn't be coming home again. We just held each other. Thank God we had a lot of support from family and friends at that time. Even to this day, it just seems like a dream but that was really the beginning of our nightmare.

'We had a wake. Aiden's body was brought home until the funeral. He spent two days and two nights at home. As the coffin was going in through our front door, there was a large crowd of people giving us support. Someone put their hand on my shoulder and said, "Don't lose your faith." I can remember saying, "That's all I've got." That was an honest-to-God answer. That was the way that I felt. That's the way I still feel two years on. I think there are things in this world that we do not understand. Maybe that's just as well. I don't know how I could cope with it otherwise.

'I personally will leave the forgiveness to God. It is very difficult to forgive people who continuously try to murder people. It's something I find difficult to deal with so I prefer to leave that. I think of Aiden and concentrate on my family rather than on those who committed the atrocity. I feel that's the only way I can cope. Not too long after the bombing, the bereaved families and some others got together because we felt that there was some comfort in numbers. That's how we support each other.

'The bomb didn't discriminate. It killed Protestants, Catholics and a Mormon family. People from every political background in Northern Ireland were affected. We decided that our politics and our religions should not be an issue. When we can come together as people who are bereaved in this way, I feel that the vast majority of people in this country should look and decide that they do not have to go through the pain that we've had to go through before they can come together. That would be the message I would send out. We really didn't need that pain. Most of us were the sort of

LOSS AND HOPE

people who had no difficulty getting on with one another. Whatever your religion or politics is, put that to one side. Our common denominator must be our Christianity and our vision of good over evil. That's probably what saved us at the end of the day.'

Forgiveness, then, was understandably a difficult concept for Michael Gallagher, as it is for many of us, but he slowly learned to shoulder his loss by remembering his son and focusing on his family in its grief. But at the same time he was able to form a community with other bereaved families and draw strength and hope from there, fired by the Christian vision that ultimately good triumphs over evil. But bereavement can affect us in different ways.

GRIEF AND GUILT

It was midnight by the time I arrived in the centre of Dublin, a matter of hours before a completely different interview on the banks of the River Liffey. Journalist Anthony Redmond greeted me off the coach and we made our way to his home on the southern side of the city. On the way he pointed out a hospital where his late mother, Nora, had prayed every day in the oratory chapel before chatting in the foyer to parents of children undergoing treatment. It was a hidden ministry of love, offering simple human kindness and reassurance.

Back at the house Anthony played a video cassette of his young-looking mother, a woman of extraordinary selflessness and charity. Anthony told me how she had died on 9 April 2003 at the age of 80. It would have been her 59th wedding anniversary. Her husband Joseph had died 27 years earlier. The Catholic writer said he still grieved for his parents and found their loss difficult to bear. But something else continued to torment him. His mother had suffered from Alzheimer's disease and, although she had asked to come home from hospital, it would not have been easy to provide the care she required, so she spent her final weeks in hospital. Anthony shoulders the guilt of not granting her that final wish.

WATERSHED

On the eighth anniversary of Nora's death in 2011, Anthony and his sister Mary travelled to the Marian shrine of Medjugorje in western Bosnia and Herzegovina, a place of pilgrimage for their mother in 1990.

'My mother was a deeply spiritual, prayerful person,' he explained. 'I would describe her temperament as contemplative and profoundly compassionate. Her spirituality was not of the holier-than-thou, sanctimonious kind but was, rather, a gentle, sensitive and loving awareness of God and the beauty of his creation. I never once heard her utter unkind words of criticism or condemnation about anyone. Indeed, if I criticised someone she would always make excuses for them and point out to me that nobody can see into another's heart but God. "There, but for the grace of God, go I," she'd say.

'She had an amazing general knowledge and took a lively interest in current affairs. She had only an old-age pension but constantly gave money to various charitable causes. I often saw her in tears as she watched reports on TV of people suffering from the effects of war or famine in other lands. On many occasions she would give me money and ask me or my sister, Mary, to go to the bank where it would be lodged in an account set up to help the victims. As a child, she and her family had known great poverty in Dublin in the late 1920s and early 1930s. She often told me stories of the suffering and hardship of those days. Then she'd add, "But, in spite of the poverty, we were happy in many ways because my mother particularly was full of love for us and she gave us very good example." Her father had also been a good man but he was somewhat more Victorian and less hands-on in his ways.'

Anthony explained how his parents had been married at St Kevin's Oratory in the famous Pro-Cathedral in Dublin towards the end of the Second World War during a time of considerable rationing. Nora spoke about her husband constantly and said how

LOSS AND HOPE

fortunate she had been to have met someone of such goodness whom she loved so deeply. They were a couple completely devoted to each other. They loved to go into town on the bus every week to shop, then have a cup of tea and perhaps a scone or, if they were in the money, an apple tart. Afterwards they'd head off to Mass in either the Pro-Cathedral or Adam and Eve's church on Merchant's Quay.

When Joseph died unexpectedly at home in the sitting room, while Nora sat talking to him, she was broken-hearted. 'I've lost my very best friend,' she told Anthony.

Yet, despite their evident happiness, they were no strangers to sadness and pain. They lost four children in infancy. It was a time, said Anthony, when many nurses, doctors and the public at large didn't show much sensitivity to a woman who had lost a new baby. In those days in Ireland, a baby who died at birth was merely taken from the mother and buried in a corner of a cemetery known as 'the plot of the angels'. When Nora's first girl died in the maternity hospital, she asked if the baby had been buried. 'Yes,' said one of the nurses coldly, 'but not in consecrated ground'. That the child had died before being baptised was something that worried Nora for years. She was constantly going to priests seeking reassurance that her daughter was with God and not in 'limbo'. The fear compounded her grief. 'Catholics are now told not to worry about limbo because it was never an essential part of the Church's teaching,' said Anthony. 'If only my poor mother could have been told that all those years ago.'

On another occasion, when Nora lost her fourth baby, also a girl, she dreaded being sent to a ward where all the other women were cradling their new-borns. A doctor, accompanied by a sister, came to speak with her and sympathised. Nora asked if she might be allowed to stay where she was, among women who had not yet had their babies. The doctor agreed immediately but, as soon as he had left, the sister upbraided Nora for daring to make the request and insisted on her being moved to the very ward she did not want to go to. 'My mother was no stranger to this kind of cruelty,' Anthony explained. 'In her usual, gentle way she'd simply ask me, "I wonder why the sister did that?"'

Anthony told me how the family had lived close to a large hospital for children. His mother loved nothing more than visiting the small, tranquil oratory every day where she would sit in silent adoration and worship. She would constantly quote Psalm 46, verse 10: 'Be still and know that I am God.' After spending time in silent prayer before the Blessed Sacrament, she would sit in the hospital foyer talking to the parents of the children. Her face would light up with the sheer joy of conversing about them. Anthony said she had an extraordinary awareness of the sacred value of children and their innocence. She loved babies, evidence to her of an infinitely good God.

When Nora was diagnosed with Alzheimer's disease, she began having severe attacks of restlessness and anxiety though her confusion was intermittent – some days she could be lucid and rational. What was most alarming was finding her walking around the house for most of the night and rarely sleeping. 'My sister and I lived with her but there was the ever-present fear that she'd fall down the stairs during the night or go to the cooker and burn herself. Visits to the hospital and to specialists in geriatric medicine were constant. It was exhausting and profoundly worrying. Some days she would get very confused and ask when she was going back to her own house. Her specialist told me she would require nursing home care and that her condition would steadily deteriorate. We resisted this as much as possible.

'At one point she went to a home, close to where we lived, for two week's respite care. The nurse asked us whether my mother was allergic to any medication so we specified the tablets she could not take. The nurse wrote this down. But when Mary and I went to visit her each day, we noticed she was heavily sedated. The policy

LOSS AND HOPE

seemed to make the home's job as easy as humanly possible by sedating the patients. One night a nurse phoned us to say they had, in error, given my mother the very medication she was allergic to and that she'd had a bad fall. By the time my sister and I got to see her, she'd had a second fall and had to be admitted to hospital where she died three months later.

'What truly breaks my heart is that my mother asked me to take her home from the hospital but I didn't because I was terrified,' Anthony confessed. 'I felt she was in good hands with professionals, doctors and nurses, who knew exactly what to do in any emergency. Mary wanted to take her home but I constantly expressed fears and serious doubts. To this very day, the guilt eats at my heart and soul. There is no peace for me. She desperately wanted to come home to be with us. She was not aware that she was dying or close to death. The fact that I didn't grant her wish fills me with the deepest anguish and guilt. Mary feels we should have done what my mother requested and she, too, feels awful pain and guilt. I felt that if we took her home against the hospital's advice they would not take her back if we needed them to. I asked whether it would be possible to take her home for even one night but was told it would be against hospital regulations and her bed could not be held for her. I cannot rid myself of the terrible feeling that I did her an injustice and, indeed, I find myself wondering whether she might have lived a bit longer if she'd come home from the hospital. I was, in fact, at my wit's end with anguish and worry. Mary kept saying that we should take her home but, to be honest, I was terrified to do so. It was a nightmare.

'In the end my mother contracted the MRSA virus and her condition got steadily worse. It was a truly dreadful time and the anguish was unbearable. We visited my mother every day and, for a few weeks before she died, were allowed to spend the night in the hospital room with her. Once she held our hands and said, "I don't want the two of you to worry about anything. I want you to have a happy life." That was the kind of unselfish, considerate woman she was.

'Shortly before she died, a commercial came on the television in her room which she watched with the sound turned down. It showed a small baby laughing. My mother opened her eyes and smiled at the baby. Her beautiful face was full of joy at the sight of the lovely baby. She remained youthful-looking even at 80. She passed away on 9 April 2003, at 8.20 in the morning. A huge part of Mary and of me went with her. She was the most saintly person I've ever known. I feel her gentle presence always with me. She made it very easy for me to believe in God. My sister Mary embodies all my mam's gentleness and transparent goodness. I hope that my mother is with my dad and her four lovely little children who went before her. When I think of my mother, the words of Thomas Gray in his *Elegy Written in a Country Churchyard* spring to mind: "Many a flower is born to blush unseen and waste its sweetness on the desert air."'

Each of us experiences loss, then, in different ways but it is always a watershed. Time may heal but we may have to learn to live with grief and regret without necessarily surmounting it. Our love becomes more vulnerable. Loss is always loss but from it new life and promise may blossom. As the German Dominican theologian Meister Eckhart noted, we grow by subtraction.

CHAPTER SEVEN
ILLUSION AND REALITY

Cinema has the power to represent some of the most pressing social and personal issues of our time, as well as all those turning points in our lives. When films succeed in making an impression. They use narrative, sound, visual space, character and symbol to experience and reflect back to us the concerns and hopes that have come to dominate a particular age or culture.

The director's representation, of course, is only one way of seeing the world, perhaps even an illusion in some people's minds of what he or she believes that truth to be. But the effect can stimulate different emotional and critical responses which connect the images on screen with a personal crisis or watershed.

When I was researching my doctorate, for example, I reached a plateau where I could not fathom the direction the thesis should take. This is not uncommon among postgraduates striving to produce an original piece of work. At something of a low ebb after years of academic research, I decided to go to the movies one afternoon at a complex near London's Marble Arch. Anthony Minghella's *The Talented Mr Ripley* happened to be showing and I entered the dark auditorium with the hope that, whatever the film was about, it might at least provide an opportunity to forget about the reality of PhD deadlines and allow me to indulge a fantasy world for a couple of hours.

But half an hour into the screening, I was dramatically brought to my senses as I suddenly realised that Minghella's masterpiece about self-identity was, in fact, precisely what I needed to explore in the thesis. It was the breakthrough that had been eluding me and there were also resonances with my deeper sense of vocation. By the time the credits were rolling, I felt I had cracked the academic code. As I walked out into the West End around teatime, I hardly knew where I was, so powerful was the film's hold on me. The borderline between illusion and reality is often blurred. As Minghella recognised, cinema creates a dream state. When you leave a cinema in the late afternoon and walk out into the street, you feel completely disorientated because reality seems much less vivid than the world in which you have just participated.

Illusion and reality can also be confused when you are wrestling with making a decision about the future. As I tried to distinguish between the two as I worked out my own future, I indulged in a certain escapism by watching movies of years gone by, only to discover a personal connection with the plot or the characters. Some of these monochromatic classics featured child stars I hadn't heard of since. With my own life possibly on a cusp, I began to wonder what future paths these young actors had taken and how they had weathered the transition.

FAME AND HUMILITY

One of them, billed as 'Bobby Henrey', had starred opposite Ralph Richardson in Carol Reed's *The Fallen Idol*, a tale about an ambassador's son called Phillipe who idolises his butler, Baines. The man is later suspected of killing his wife after she accidentally falls down the stairs. It was a powerful performance by an 8-year-old and, as Bobby had clearly not stayed in cinema, I embarked on some research. Little then did I imagine the blond-haired boy with a slight French accent had gone on to become a married deacon in the Roman Catholic Church

I managed to trace the Reverend Robert Henrey to a town in

ILLUSION AND REALITY

Connecticut where, at the age of 72, he was about to retire as a chaplain at Greenwich Hospital. Through email correspondence, he told me how he had been born in a quaint medieval farmhouse in Normandy (which he still visits) but moved with his near penniless parents to London in the early years of the war. His father, a journalist, got a government job writing war-related stories but, constantly broke, decided to turn to writing. One of his books, *A Village in Piccadilly*, happened to include several photographs of his son. The book came into the hands of a member of a film crew adapting a Graham Greene short story, *The Basement Room*, for the big screen. Producers were on the look-out for a juvenile lead and thought Bobby might be perfect for the role.

'They sent a private plane to nearby Deauville airport to pick me up,' Robert recalled. 'The only thing I remember was the thrill of flying for the first time – the views from the little plane as it banked over the Normandy fields and headed north over the Channel, the din of the engines and the smell of petrol. What did I know or care about film-making! I do remember a meeting in a swank office around Marble Arch overlooking Hyde Park. I assume that both Alexander Korda, the owner of London Films, and Carol Reed were there but I must have been far more interested in the strangeness of the setting – the wood panelling and the high ceilings – to give much thought to the names of those who were talking to me. Anyway, after that, my mother told me we would be spending a lot more time in London and that it had something to do with this film business.'

Ralph Richardson, Michèle Morgan and other cast members, including Jack Hawkins, had been perfectly friendly to him but in a professional, distant way. However, Sonia Dresdel (who paradoxically played the part of a mean housekeeper bent on vengeance) was by far the warmest. Robert lived with his mother in a residential suite that formed part of the studio facilities. He also had a governess. He remembered Carol Reed as a fine director who had

WATERSHED

probably needed a great deal of patience to deal with his own inquisitive nature. Rather than constraining the young Bobby to do things his own way, Reed would observe him, then encourage him to act in accordance with his innate mannerisms.

The ending of his brief film career after eight months ushered in a watershed as he was sent to a Benedictine boarding school where he had to fend for himself among children his own age. 'That transition was neither easy nor particularly pleasant,' he recollected. 'I coped by putting the whole experience to one side and pretending to myself it had never happened. That wasn't very realistic but was, I suppose, understandable. It was difficult for me to go back to living a normal life. Young people don't like to be different – the peer pressure is real. That was painful. I had been the only child on the set. That did not make me feel lonely because I was used to the company of adults but later I realised that it had caused me to be different. This was reinforced by the fact that I was an only child, that from 1940 to 1945 I lived in central London where, due to the war, there were no children, and that to make things worse my parents had odd ideas about educating me at home rather than at school.'

The celebrity status contributed to those feelings of isolation. 'I would like to think that it did not go to my head. That said, I couldn't help being aware of my special status. People would stop me in the street and sort of gawk – there were endless interviews and picture-taking. My parents – my mother in particular – liked all this. I think I was bemused more than anything else, but we humans are naturally quite vain. Some of this must have percolated through into my psyche. As an adult I would describe myself as a rather private person who is not good at schmoozing and who dislikes being schmoozed. Fame – like the illusion of power – is a potent brew with complex side-effects.

'Early on I got the message that the stage is in some ways more

ILLUSION AND REALITY

real than reality, and that story, metaphor and ritual are enormously important to our understanding of life: an essential lens through which to sharpen our understanding. I think this is what good religious practice and ritual are all about. Ministry in a religious context is associated with taking on a part.

'I'd like to think that when all is said and done it taught me humility: this is something that happened to me to a large extent by chance. It was actually a good thing and it was important to do it to the best of my ability, but it was a gift – gifts can be hugely complex and confusing things to deal with. Above all, they need to be accepted with humility, otherwise things can go seriously wrong.'

Much to the discomfort of his Protestant family, Robert later became a Roman Catholic. He says Gregorian chant attracted him to Catholicism and his Benedictine teachers helped him win a place to Oxford where he met his wife and was also fortunate in having a tutor who taught him to enjoy reading and encouraged him to discover different languages. Far from the realm of movie-making, Robert entered the world of chartered accountancy, living in Asia, Latin America and the United States. He became a partner in one of the large accounting firms in New York, and was involved in corporate tax work.

Robert had always been interested in religion and had long been aware of his contemplative nature. Had he not married young, he might have been drawn towards a monastic vocation. To this day, he feels rooted in Benedictine spirituality. When he was 40, Robert and his wife moved back to New York after living in Singapore. They had two young children and knew it was time to settle down. Although committed to an extremely demanding career, he wanted to set limits. He knew that, since Vatican II, the Roman Catholic Church had been willing to ordain married men as deacons. So he decided to offer himself. The training involved three years of part-time theological study and a willingness to make a lifelong

WATERSHED

commitment. Ordained in 1984, Robert was assigned to his local parish in Connecticut, but also found himself gravitating towards hospital ministry.

'It was part-time, obviously, since I was taking the train into Manhattan every weekday to earn a living,' he explained. 'It was a good experience from the beginning – none of my partners ever objected to my having committed myself to doing something outside the firm. When I retired at the relatively young age of 58, I still had enough energy to move into a second career. Over two years I embarked on a series of clinical internships in hospitals leading to certification as a chaplain. That enabled me to get a professional job with a hospital, ministering not just to Catholics but to all patients. The training was challenging and enriching with an emphasis on psychology, mental health and working with all religious traditions. I'm now 72 and about to retire for a second time. I hope, however, to have enough energy to stay with my parish, preaching and helping out generally. It's an emotionally supportive environment and I feel lucky.'

Robert's wife, Lisette, is English but he remains deeply rooted in his French background, pointing out that 45 years of living in the United States has not diminished that. The couple had two children, Dominique and Edward, but, shortly before her nineteenth birthday, Dominique (a talented young woman who would have become a professional writer) died from an allergic reaction while she was in her first year at Columbia University. 'We knew she had a serious allergy to peanuts,' Robert explained. 'We were on vacation at Christmas and she died from anaphylactic shock after drinking a cup of chocolate – it must have contained traces of peanut. This happened in 1988 and had a profound impact on my life, my wife's and my son's – we were all together when it happened. It was devastating. Edward was 15 at the time.

'One of life's lessons is that intense pain takes each of us on a highly personal journey – we're alone with it and have to muddle through in the hope that the sunshine will one day make its way back into our lives. It's the loneliness of it that makes us so vulnerable to giving up on our relationships. My wife and I were spared that – we made it through together. When eventually I did make it through recovery, the fact that I was a deacon helped me listen to the pain of others ... and that was a privilege. None of us wants to experience pain – that kind of pain should be avoided at all cost. But the reality is that pain, however unwelcome, is a powerful teacher.'

ART OF THE CINEMA

Robert Henrey was not the only former child star to come into my orbit. Dr Jon Whiteley, senior assistant keeper of the Ashmolean Museum of Art and Archaeology in Oxford, is a noted art historian and a Presbyterian. But as a schoolboy he, too, faced a watershed when he was taken out of the classroom and onto the film set. The BBC had been visiting schools in Aberdeenshire, interviewing children and asking them to perform. John had recited a poem which impressed a talent scout looking for a boy to play opposite Dirk Bogarde in *Hunted*, a film about the flight of a criminal from London to the north of Scotland where he steals a boat and makes his way out to sea. Summoned for a screen test, Jon got the part and spent a childhood in front of the camera.

'My mother supported me up to a point but also protected me,' he recalled. 'My parents weren't at all keen on the prospect of my going into films, even though my mother had been very involved with amateur theatricals as a producer of plays. They were very doubtful about allowing me to take the part at all. In the end they decided that it might be good if an unruly 6-year-old were thrown into an adult world and taught some sense.

'Acting amused me. But I always knew from an early age that

WATERSHED

it was going to end when I was 11. This was part of the bargain. It was my parents who decided that, come the 11-plus, school was going to take over. They were also very reluctant to allow me to do more than one film a year so other offers were turned down with some regularity, rather to the annoyance of my agent who lost by it, of course.'

Jon was always enthralled by the mechanics of film-making, remembering the back projection and the smell of the set, a cocktail of carbon and wood chippings. The arc lights gave off a distinctive aroma which blended with that of the freshly cut woods for the interiors. But the established star meant nothing to him at all, although he and Bogarde were to become close. 'He was like an elder brother and he was great fun. He was always bringing me presents and inviting me out to tea. He was very protective and very charming. I enjoyed his company very much and I liked acting with him. We did have a kind of relationship in the film which certainly helped the end product.'

Jon went on to win an Oscar for his second major movie, *The Kidnappers*, about two children who find a baby abandoned in the woods and keep her as a pet. It also starred Duncan Macrae, Jean Anderson and Adrienne Corri. The award eventually arrived by post in a wooden box in which Jon later kept his Matchbox toys. His mother didn't feel it was worth going out to Hollywood. They didn't know in advance that he would win and the invitation was, to his parents' way of thinking at least, a distraction from academic endeavours.

A contract to appear in *Moonfleet*, directed by Fritz Lang, necessitated four months in Hollywood, even though the gothic melodrama about smugglers and pirates was set in southern England. Jon played a young orphan sent to a Dorset village to stay with an old friend of his mother, an elegant but morally ambiguous character brought to the screen by Stewart Granger. 'Working with

ILLUSION AND REALITY

Fritz Lang was like working with Michelangelo,' Jon revealed. 'I was in the presence of somebody who was a powerful artist but with no respect at all for actors. He liked things done the way he envisaged them and became very upset indeed if he didn't get what he wanted. And it was sometimes hard to know what he wanted because he didn't explain it very clearly. His idea of direction, unlike other directors I had worked with, was to take two steps forward, one step to the left, look up and then you said your lines. This was about all you got from him and, if you didn't deliver what he wanted on top of that, then he used to become really very upset, not only with me but the other actors as well – and with the chippies and people on set. I think children are more likely to forgive the frailties of adults than other adults and that was certainly the case. I had sympathy for him. I admired him as an artist. He was himself an artist. He used to draw off set and, as I had ambitions also to be an artist it was a bond between us.

'From a very early age I had wanted to be a painter, and cinema seemed to me a creation very similar to the art of painting. Many of the people I worked with, including Dirk Bogarde, were artists and they brought a sense of artistry to what they did which I liked. It was entirely intuitive. It comes from being a certain age when you learn things on the job and respond to things as they come. It is a learning process as my parents always hoped it would be and indeed it was.

'I wasn't even allowed to stay on the set in case there was something psychologically disturbing being filmed. I was furious at being removed on the grounds that this might be harmful to me. I knew differently. There were also the real accidents that occurred on set, particularly in a film like *Moonfleet* where there was a great deal of fighting between stunt men.

'I remember there was a scene in which a man was hanging in a gibbet. It was pretty grim but I didn't mind. Then I noticed that,

WATERSHED

while he was in the gibbet, his face was turning a different colour, He was made up to look like a corpse but he became more and more corpse-like in reality and, after a moment, I realised there was something wrong – the wire around his waist had slipped and the rope was throttling him. He was taken off to hospital unconscious.'

Jon starred again with Dirk Bogarde in *The Spanish Gardener*. Shot at Pinewood and at S'Agaro on the Costa Brava, it told the story of a minor diplomat (Michael Hordern) who becomes increasingly jealous of the relationship between his son (Whiteley) and the hired gardener (Bogarde). 'Meeting Dirk for the first time in five years was an entirely different experience,' Jon told me. 'I was older and I think I felt my age at that time. Twelve-year-olds become prigs and are much more self-aware than six-year-olds. I felt at the time that I had somehow outgrown Dirk and, although I was looking forward to meeting him again, I felt a difference in his character. He had become sharper, more self-aware, and a little more difficult in his dealings with people round about him, which I didn't entirely care for. The two of us had changed and I felt disappointed at that time.

'People who were actors of distinction struck me as people who were colleagues and friends of mine, not people who were famous, becoming famous or important. They were people who inhabited a world that was my world, in a way that the normal world was not. I wasn't aware of the difference. I had a rapport with that other world. I felt at home with actors. I liked their company and felt we had something in common. I didn't think they were any different from me or the world at large. When I was very young, I think Dirk did treat me like a son or a nephew. When I was a little older, there was a certain distance between us which didn't exist in that way before. When I was 6 he would buy me toys all the time. When I was 12 he bought me wristwatches more befitting my station in life. It defined the difference between us across the years.'

When Jon returned obediently to the classroom at the age of

ILLUSION AND REALITY

11, inevitably he began to miss the movie world. 'I knew that a shutter had come down and that I wouldn't go back to it. I also missed things I hadn't realised I would miss, like having a chauffeur, which I took for granted. Suddenly I realised I was never again going to have a driver and a large black saloon to take me around shopping.'

He went on: 'My mother put me in the cinema with great hesitation, reluctance and uncertainty which she never relinquished. As I grow older, it seems to me more of a whole than it may have seemed at the time. As an art historian, an early training in speaking in the cinema and a sense of rhetoric, has spread into one's speaking skills to large audience with clarity and clear diction.'

Jon Whiteley sees modern cinema as being the heir of the great artistic traditions of the past, claiming there are no longer painters or sculptors of worth. The great traditions have passed away but it is cinema that keeps the artistic flame alive. Like the old masters, the new movies speak to a broad audience base. As an art historian, he regards the cinema as being part of the world he now inhabits. Cinema is an art form, he says, the great narrative art of our time, communicating through images, messages and stories that appeal to people at large.

Artists in previous centuries who painted the crucifixion, or other scenes of religious art, were not creating great works of art to be admired for their aesthetic value, he explained. They were producing images with a relevance to the purpose they were intended to serve. Unlike what he terms 'the ambiguity and obscurantism' of modern painting and sculpture, art of the past prized clarity. It embodied a language intended to speak to the eye. Paintings shrouded in mystery were less common than pictures that told a lucid story, dependent of course on a well-known narrative understandable to the observers.

Dr Whiteley believes the search for novelty in painting has had a calamitous effect on the nature of art. Art exists in a tradition, the denial of which has had catastrophic consequences for the nature of contemporary art. Art is convention. It is like nature. You can't dispense with it, he says. Art is not a science that can be tested against a set of proposals experimentally and then found to fall by the wayside. It is something much more open-minded, something existing in a tradition. As soon as you break that tradition, then art is lost.

The purpose of art, as the American art historian Bernard Berenson once put it, is to enhance lives. 'And it does,' says Jon Whiteley. 'Without it we would all be very much the poorer. You only have to go to a church in a Catholic country to see how people respond to its paintings. It is very different from how the art historian responds. Mothers who have lost her children respond to images of the Virgin Mary, such as the Pietà, in a way that is extremely personal to them. I am very moved by the spectacle of people in Catholic churches who are treating the images in the way that they are intended to be treated, not necessarily as great art. This is one of the great conundrums for an art historian – that it doesn't require what we think of as "great art" to move people in a way that "great art" ought.

'People will get out of a picture things that an artist may not have intended them to take from that picture. A religious artist may paint a picture because he or she is deeply religious: the image that comes out at the other end is a religious picture. Another artist might paint a picture that is indistinguishable from this work of art but that person might be an atheist and be doing it for the money. The motive of the artist is as diverse as the response of the people looking at these paintings. There is no such thing as a unified response.'

It might seem surprising in today's celebrity culture to read of two child actors who could have gone on to become box office names in the cinema but instead took their final bows at an early

ILLUSION AND REALITY

age and never looked back. They found not fame but fulfilment in other avenues far from the glare of the studio lights. It might have seemed to some on the sound stage that those young performers were destined for stardom. But that would have been only a dream as future reality was to prove.

We all have illusions about ourselves and expectations of others. Living a spiritual life is often about distinguishing between image and reality. As I reflected on what might lie ahead of me, I learned from the one-time child stars that we are not necessarily defined for ever by something that marks us out at an earlier stage of our lives. And as I will describe in the next chapter, it was a religious work of art that was to have a subtle but unexpected effect on my midlife transition.

CHAPTER EIGHT
STRUGGLE AND FAITH

Sometimes we reach our turn in the road during daylight. The route ahead is boldly signposted and we know the direction we must take. But there are also times when the way forward is unclear, shrouded and laden with anxiety.

Yet often it is only by entering the darkness and losing our bearings that we discover the way. The Benedictine writer Joan Chittister has even said that darkness deserves gratitude, for through it we learn to understand that all growth does not take place in the sunlight.

Whatever darkness means to us personally, it is an ongoing spiritual process in which we are liberated from compulsions and empowered to love more freely. The darkness of the night might make us feel vulnerable but it implies nothing sinister, only that the release from our obsessions may happen in secret without our needing to know or understand.

Nonetheless, whatever we are having to deal with in our lives, the dark night of the soul can also bestow unexpected blessings and new insights.

FACING FEAR

We can be friends with someone all our life, but never really know them. Yet, we can also become friends with someone in their final weeks and feel we have known them for a lifetime. One blustery day in September 2010, I travelled to the Wirral in northern Britain

STRUGGLE AND FAITH

to meet the author Grace Sheppard, who told me that she had recently received her third cancer diagnosis and things were not good. Through my brief friendship over the next two months, I learnt much about the mystery of love and suffering. The outer engagement allowed an inner journey to be shared and celebrated, one which touched the depths of human and spiritual experience.

As a spiritual writer, Grace Sheppard had written honestly about her experience of fear and faith without being sentimental. In her book, *An Aspect of Fear*, she described how days after her wedding to the England test cricketer, the Reverend David Sheppard (later to become the Anglican Bishop of Liverpool), a short illness triggered desperate fears which made her afraid of leaving the safety of her own home.[13]

During our initial conversation, Grace was radiant as she talked about the positive ways in which she had embraced the fear of facing a terminal diagnosis a matter of years after she had nursed her husband through cancer.

'Gratitude should bubble out of us,' she enthused. 'I have such wonderful friends who've offered help to me in my present state of health which makes me feel well and makes me want to live. It makes me bubble over with this joy of life which I know other people are picking up. It's unselfconscious but it's real. I think very often the people who are helping me have themselves been helped and so there's a chain of this gratitude turning into goodness and healing.

'There's a huge power in gratitude. I think it could change the world. Being thankful is much deeper than just being polite. I look over there and see pictures of my grandsons and my daughter, flowers that somebody has brought me, a drink that will help me quench my thirst, all these little things, and they mount up. I think, "My goodness, aren't I lucky? Aren't I blessed?" To me these are all gifts from God. You simply have to say thank you and it turns into worship in a natural kind of way.

WATERSHED

'I can only speak about my experience of suffering and, as you know, I have had three diagnoses of cancer. I have survived forty-five years since the first one, four years since the second one and now I am in the throes of a third. Yes I have been suffering, but it depends how able you are, I think it depends how loved you are – and perhaps how loved you have been – as to whether you are able to find a positive way through this. I have seen and heard so many people with cancer who are feeling negative, and I would never, ever blame them for that. I would feel very sad for them but I can only say that I have been given a gift of seeing that the glass is half-full and not half-empty. That's why I go on being thankful. And it does help the suffering. It helps you do the hard bits. It helps you get through the pain. It helps you get through the confusion. It helps you get through the things you have to get through in hospital and in waiting rooms and so on. I hope that in some way my experience of this will help perhaps just one other person to find a positive way through because we're all faced with a fork in the road, aren't we? We make choices and for me I have seen self-pity in people and I don't like it, and therefore I don't want to go there. And so if that crops up at my fork in the road, I will look at that and say, "No I don't want to go down there. I am going to go down the other way and try to work my way down that way." But it comes back to gratitude – that's the key: this awareness of gifts and of love. And I have had a lot of love in my life and that's helped me to handle the suffering that I have to handle at the moment.'

Grace's final days were spent in a hospice where she shared with her daughter Jenny the experience of feeling she was 'hovering between two worlds'. There was a pulling in both directions but it was clear that she wanted to move to the next world. Despite difficulties with her breathing, Grace told Jenny that dying was nothing to be afraid of. In fact, she felt distinct excitement and could discern 'something wonderful' about what was about to happen. In the

STRUGGLE AND FAITH

consoling atmosphere of the hospice, Jenny felt that dying was no more fearful than being born.

It was my brief friendship with Grace, I think, that allowed me to let go of anxiety and, once and for all, move towards a decision I knew I would have to make. As the nights began to draw in that autumn, I found myself battling real inner fear about making that step. I felt vulnerable. The fading landscape all around me did little to lift my spirits even though I could discern a beauty in decay. Perhaps the shedding of the leaves and the stripping bare of the trees symbolised a process I, too, had to face. As Grace's condition worsened, I found myself entering a tunnel where I pondered my own mortality and, more especially, the mortality of all those I love, with a morbid fixation which locked me in a room without light or hope. Such was the experience of dereliction that at times eternity seemed to hold no meaning at all. I wanted to flee but was forced to stay in the darkness and confront the fears – one by one.

Salvation came initially through the words of a wise spiritual companion who pointed out that each of us needs light and dark in our lives – too much of either isn't a healthy thing. She told me to remember that as the sun was setting here in England, it was rising somewhere else on the other side of the world. Befriend the outer darkness, she said, and face the darkness within.

And so I did. Tentatively at first, upheld by the words of St Augustine of Hippo: 'Light of my heart, do not let my darkness speak to me.'

In the end, it was art that pulled me through. Ever since I studied the history of art at university, I've believed in the transformative power of painting. I had in the attic a large framed print of Holman Hunt's *The Light of the World*. It had never been a great favourite because I had seen reproductions of it everywhere, so I was slightly surprised to find myself desiring it so urgently. An allegory on the text from the Book of Revelation, 'Behold I stand at the door and knock', it depicts the sad face of the waiting Christ carrying a lamp. On his head are two crowns – the earthly crown of shame and the heavenly halo of glory. Sometime later I discovered that Holman Hunt had made the thorny crown begin to bud and blossom and so, living and sleeping alongside that image over the ensuing weeks, I gradually came to accept the darkness, not as a time of despair, but as an invitation to summon courage.

After meditating alongside *The Light of the World*, I was eventually able to make a decision I had been postponing. But it seemed I had needed to sustain an absence of light in order to trust the road ahead.

St John of the Cross says that God darkens our awareness (which may create a misplaced sense of fear) in order to keep us safe.

LIVING WITH DOUBT

Now canon treasurer of St Paul's Cathedral in London, Mark Oakley was rector of the actors' church, St Paul's, in Covent Garden, when we first met. That day he described a watershed moment in his own life which eventually led to his writing a popular paperback, *The Collage of God*.[14]

Just before he was ordained, Mark had been sent by his theological college on a pastoral placement to St Mary's Hospital, Paddington. 'I suppose I encountered there experiences I had never had before,' he told me. 'I remember a very painful day when I was asked to go and see a young man, the same age as me, who was dying. He had literally an hour or two left to live. I was asked to sit with him as he died. I recall that I was really unable to tie this up at all with my faith in God because I saw not only his excruciating pain as he died but also his parents' pain at losing their son. It collapsed my thinking. I didn't have anything else to stand on afterwards for quite a while. I suppose, in retrospect, what happened was that I

STRUGGLE AND FAITH

had to rethink my faith, but at the time it felt like an abyss. It had all gone. I couldn't see the point any more. I couldn't see God. My faith felt like a sham. I just felt very alone and almost despairing.

'About two weeks after this encounter with the young man, I decided that I didn't want to be ordained. I even started to look at the job pages of newspapers. Then, gradually, friends started to talk to me realistically and helpfully, and I started to think that perhaps I could re-imagine a faith and God. But I was going to need a lot of help.'

Reading the first chapter of *The Collage of God*, I was struck by Mark Oakley's claim that, on the whole, religious people fall into two basic categories. On the one hand, there are those who want to resolve the mystery of God ... 'to be like a reporting journalist ("our God correspondent") and relay information in black and white language to those in "the know". On the other, there are those who, instead of wanting to resolve the mystery, seek to deepen it, coming to believe that truth is not the same thing as the elimination of ambiguity.'

I understood what Mark Oakley meant about reporters – that, by and large, journalists do approach matters of faith like believers with a scientific (and sometimes even fundamentalist) mindset, simplifying complexity for the sake of clarity and reaching a conclusion that might effectively overlook a matrix of nuance. But in my bones I felt that my own journalistic experience of being alongside people during or after their liminal times had actually been a conduit for deepening that mystery, not resolving it, and therefore I had been reluctant to move away from the profession.

At the time of the publication of *The Collage of God*, I interviewed Dr Rowan Williams (then Archbishop of Wales) about his impressions of the book. For him it was about trying to believe in God seriously and, moreover, for that belief to make a difference. 'If you understand a bit about how icons in the Eastern Church work, you'll see that they all prescribe a kind of journey,' he told me at his home in Newport. 'Icons draw your eyes around in a pattern. They don't deliver all at once. They oblige you to take time looking. You see with the heart. In that process, you discover who and what you are. And it can't be rushed. There are no shortcuts.'

The Archbishop said he believed that faith constantly moved in and out of being a collage and a creed. 'If you just have collage, there's always the danger of self-indulgence,' he said. 'There's got to be some underlying shape, some real substance. But, equally, because faith is something that takes time, the collage approach is hugely important. If you read the New Testament, there's a collage there before there's a creed. An exceptionally important point about Christian faith is that it begins with that plurality (and even messiness of witness) before it settles down into being a creed. Unless you have something of that sense of richness and variety, you'll never get to the creed or not in any sense that makes the creed mean anything.

'In the fourth century, when the creeds are finalised – the main documents anyway – you find an increasing suspicion of formulation and an increasing concern with what you can't say about God, with the negative and the mystical, and these just go hand in hand very naturally. The more you're being precise about things, the more perhaps you need to remind yourself that you don't have it wrapped up.'

For Rowan Williams, the search for what one can trust is utterly inseparable from the life of faith. 'If you look at some of the great literature of the spiritual struggle across the centuries, then the way in which the formulations lose their sense and their conviction is very much part of your journey into, not out of, faith. It requires that you look for your energy for trust deeper and deeper down in your self all the time, and say, "well it doesn't depend on *that*, it doesn't depend on *that*, it doesn't depend on *that*", until you finally get to that darkest point that St John of the Cross writes about where really

STRUGGLE AND FAITH

all you can do is just say, "I'm not sure if I trust anything but I do want to" – and hang on by your fingernails to that and hope that the world will reassemble around you; that beneath that deepest and darkest point, there's still the hand of God.'

WRESTLING WITH BELIEF

The French film actress Juliette Binoche was a teenager at a Catholic school in Paris when she first visited the ecumenical community of Taizé in Burgundy. She was 13 when she went with her sister, and 15 when she returned on pilgrimage with fellow students. After the tragic death of the community's founder, Brother Roger, I flew to Paris where the star of *The English Patient*, *Chocolat* and *Breaking and Entering* had agreed to speak to me about the influence of Taizé on her young life.

'I felt like I was being accepted as I was – good or bad, having faith or not having faith,' she recalled. 'There was something about allowing myself to be who I was, not knowing who I was exactly. I remember the immense warmth when we sang all together. Brother Roger was rehearsing the songs with us and there was a kindness there, just by the way he was talking to us. It felt like it was a personal relationship, that he was talking only to you.'

For Juliette Binoche the experience provided an immense feeling of protection, fulfilling a need of community without religious affiliation. It was concerned with *being*. 'That's where I found a sort of a treasure somehow and what I remember is the infinite feeling of love. That is a sort of a reference for me. If, in the future, I had to play a nun, I would refer myself to that period of time, having the feeling in your heart of this infinite love that you can feel sometimes in loving someone.'

Taizé had been a watershed. 'It was a time of inner growth with a lot of teenage questions, not necessarily with a need of answers, but the questions needed to be heard and put down on the table – all the conflicts and the knowledge, realising that somebody knows the text, inviting you to a reflection and to find your own path somehow.'

To convey the impression the community had made on her, the actress began to hum a Taizé chant that had stayed with her like a mantra for more than twenty years. There had been something about the melody and rhythm that had proved healing to body and soul, providing 'an inner softness' where the chant could inhabit her. This experience had brought peace and less judgement both on her and on others. Furthermore, the mystery of the chant had been an instrumental factor in her process of maturity.

'I haven't been back since I was 15 but it is still in me,' she said. 'It's like when you've seen an amazing horizon. A beautiful sunset always stays in you, no matter how many years have passed. There is something about that with Taizé when you see the infinite somehow.'

Brother Roger believed it wasn't necessary to see clearly on the journey of faith before pronouncing a 'yes' to Christ. Lucidity came with trust and, through the affirmation, a new life of creativity and freedom. Even Brother Roger had doubts from time to time. They formed part of his faith journey. The darker the shadows became, he said, the more a person could discover the delight of believing. Belief necessarily embraced a consenting to the night. To refuse one's night would be to seek a privilege. If we could see on our journey of faith as we can in broad daylight, he would say, what purpose would believing serve?

The thoughts of Grace Sheppard, Mark Oakley, Rowan Williams, Juliette Binoche and Brother Roger of Taizé suggest that living through darkness, ambiguity and uncertainty need not be a disintegrating experience but one which can lead us to the loving mercy of God which manifests itself in unexpected places and often when we least expect it.

Struggle and faith are inseparable.

CHAPTER NINE
ABANDONMENT AND TRUST

There are times when we have to let go and let God. Death is, of course, the ultimate threshold but there are smaller deaths throughout life which prepare us for this final watershed. The French Catholic writer Father Jean-Pierre de Caussade says complete and utter abandonment to the will of God is the essence of spirituality. De Caussade believes we are sent along the path chosen for us even though we cannot see it and have nothing to rely on except divine guidance kept secret from us. God's action is always new and fresh. It never retraces its steps, but finds new routes.

> It is no use trying to see where we are, look at maps, or question passers-by. That would not be tolerated by a guide who wants us to rely on him. He will get satisfaction from overcoming our fears and doubts, and will insist that we have complete trust in him.[15]

In his classic text, *Abandonment to Divine Providence*, de Caussade persuades us of the necessity of loving God beyond all else by completely surrendering ourselves to him. This submission does not demand heroic feats or pious devotions. The way of pure faith enables us to become aware of the hidden God and all that is necessary in the sacrament of the present moment, and in the most humble and unlikely situations. Nothing is too trivial for God who is always closer to us than we think. Holiness is simply about complete

WATERSHED

loyalty to the will of God which leads to peace and joy. When people give themselves entirely to God, their lives become sermons.

De Caussade draws on artistic metaphors in suggesting that we offer ourselves to God 'like a clean, smooth canvas'. We do not have to worry about what God may choose to paint on it, 'for we have perfect trust in him, have abandoned ourselves to him, and are so busy doing our duty that we forget ourselves and all our needs'. Each blow from the hammer of the sculptor's chisel makes a lump of stone feel – if it could – as if it were being destroyed. As blow after blow descends, the stone knows nothing of how the sculptor is shaping it.[16]

Those in whom God lives are often 'flung into a corner like a useless bit of broken pottery'. He goes on: 'There they lie, forsaken by everyone, but yet enjoying God's very real and active love and knowing they have to do nothing but stay in his hands and be used as he wishes.'[17] The world thinks them useless and so they appear, says the Jesuit priest, but through concealed channels they pour out spiritual help without ever realising.

Likewise, argues de Caussade, we may feel that, after we have given ourselves to God, we are being ruined and disfigured by the master sculptor but all we have to do is to concentrate on the present moment, think only of our duty, and suffer all that is inflicted without knowing the purpose or fretting about it.

RESISTANCE AND DESIRE

The book was instrumental in my decision to offer myself as a candidate for ordination in the Anglican Church.

Several months later, towing my case on wheels along the railway platform en route to a national selection conference, my eye caught fleeting sight of the headlines on a newspaper stand. My mind went back to the day my first exclusive hit the placards. I was going to miss that world but believed the time had come to abandon it, if the church discerned that too. In an age of tweeting and

ABANDONMENT AND TRUST

blogging, I felt like an old man recalling nostalgic youth. But the profession had changed and so had I.

The personal nature of journalism had always been more gratifying than scoops and bylines, pursued though these were with relentless desire. Since the age of 19, when I entered an editorial noviciate on the Torbay coast, I had been crossing the threshold of other people's homes, entering into the joys and sorrows of many different lives.

Priests do this too. But the rite of ordination was something I had always resisted, even though I had found myself thinking about it all the time. My bookshelves, laden with tomes on ordained ministry and pastoral care, told their own story. They had been a constant mirror of a world to which I felt curiously drawn but reluctant to embrace. The spectre of holy orders was something I dreaded, yet also longed for at the same time. I was content to live with the paradox for as long as I could – or dared. In the past I had twice been recommended for training and both times I decided not to see it through. The timing had not been right, even though there were those in ecclesiastical circles who felt I was abandoning my vocation to be a priest.

Stories about people resisting ordination have long appealed to me.

There are tales of desert monks from the fourth and fifth centuries retreating further and further into the Egyptian wilderness when they got wind that episcopal eyes were on the look-out for men to be ordained. They knew that becoming a priest would sound the death knell to their life of contemplation.

In the fourth century, Gregory Nazianzen was ordained much against his will by his father, the Bishop of Nazianzus. But Gregory abandoned his father's church and returned to monastic solitude where, in time, he came to regret his escape and accepted that he had received a divine call to priesthood, in spite of the forcible way it had been administered. He still had to face the flock and defend his actions in words which became an influential series of meditations on the responsibility and privilege of priesthood.

When, as a deacon, John Chrysostom received wind that he and his friend were to be promoted 'to the dignity of the priesthood' in Antioch, he was overcome not only with fear that he, too, would be seized against his will but also with bewilderment that he could possibly be considered worthy of the honour. The pair agreed they had to decide together whether to escape or be taken. John knew his friend's keenness but was all too aware of his own reluctance as well as the certainty that he would be blamed if his own weakness deprived the flock of Christ of a good man. John writes that when 'the one who was to ordain us had come, I remained in hiding, while he, knowing nothing of this, was taken off on some other pretext. He submitted to the yoke, expecting from my promises to him that I too should certainly follow, or rather, thinking that he was following me ... But when he heard that I had escaped, he came to me in great dejection and sat by my side.'[18]

This time, though, it seemed different. I remembered the wisdom of a brother at Taizé who had counselled me many years before: 'Without abandoning something, you might not be able to enter something else,' he had told me, recalling how a French journalist had become a priest much later in life. 'Vocation is personal. There might come a day when the desire to become a priest proves overwhelming. Don't think too much about it but, if it becomes too strong, you should do it. You will be given back the things you will lose. But it is important to wait. It might be wrong to force yourself into work which is not right. Don't accuse yourself. Have the courage to wait until it has become simple. If it is to be sacramental priesthood, you will know. Oscillation is a sign of complication. Priesthood requires abandonment. You need to be free in order to give freely. Give thanks for what has been given today and the work you do. Find joy in that. God has not abandoned you. He has carried you.'

ABANDONMENT AND TRUST

So here I was, in the small cathedral city of Ely, dragging my luggage towards a selection panel, all too aware that, were I to be recommended as a full-time candidate, it would spell the end of my reporting days – and that would be the biggest turning point in my life.

Yet now, in the warm sunshine of an afternoon in May, my feelings were not those of despondency but of confidence, hope and joy. To be an ordained priest in the church was truly my heart's desire. I could no longer deny it – neither to myself nor to anyone else. After many years of resistance, it seemed I had crossed a psychological barrier or, to put it more anthropologically, had been through a rite of passage.

However, as a previous book, *Song of the Nightingale*, recounted, for many years my life had already seemed to have taken on a 'priestly' character.[19] It was not only the fact that my work dispatched me to a galaxy of human situations to be alongside others at liminal times, and to challenge hypocrisy and injustices in the church and society, but also the truth that, like every other Christian pilgrim, I had opportunities to minister quietly without the need of a collar. Furthermore, I was not convinced that God envisaged me as the public office-holder of a particular denomination. Journalists cross boundaries (and build bridges) with frequent ease and, as an ecumenical lay person, I imitated my professional liberties without shame or compunction.

I found theological corroboration in the writings of Sister Jean-Marie Howe, former abbess of the Trappestine Abbey of Notre-Dame de l'Assomption, Rogersville, New Brunswick, Canada, who sent me both the English and French editions of her first book, *Spiritual Journey: The Monastic Way*.[20] The little blue paperback defines the spiritual life as a journey based on our innate capacity for God, one which is awakened and developed through immersion in the Mystery of Christ, facilitated by an assimilation of the Word of God, which can ultimately lead to a transformation of being.

WATERSHED

Writing with monastics in mind, the author argues that we are on a journey which transforms and can ultimately create in us a state of spiritual being that finds its origin through deep participation in the life of Christ. At this deepest level of spiritual life, writes Sister Jean-Marie, our being, now united to Christ's, becomes a channel of grace which saves and heals the world. This is sanctity – no longer 'I' but Christ that lives in me, and this life of Christ in me transforms the world.

The monk is characterised by emptiness, born of the 'consuming desire' of the Spirit dwelling in our heart. Just as we cannot really fill ourselves, so we cannot really empty ourselves. Immersion in the Mystery of Christ both fills and empties. She cites the image of an immobile incenser – its emptiness is filled with incense that wafts out of it into the surrounding atmosphere. Equally, we could speak of the incense of spiritual being pouring out of the monk's emptiness into the world in adoration and intercession. For Jean-Marie Howe, the image symbolises a 'spiritual priesthood'. Capacity, kenosis, rebirth, spiritual being – all lead not only to personal transformation in Christ but also to a cosmic transformation of the entire Body of Christ.

The notion of 'spiritual priesthood' took on a deeper meaning after Sister Jean-Marie read Graham Greene's *The Power and the Glory*. Set in southern Mexico during an anti-clerical purge, the novel follows a priest who has lost everything because of his human failings, yet whose frailty does not hamper his fidelity and passion for the exercises of his priestly functions, notably saying Mass and hearing confession, which Howe claims as the power and the glory.

But as well as sacramental wine and sacramental priesthood, there is another wine – the wine of spiritual being – and another priesthood, the spiritual priesthood, which embodies what it means to be an intermediary between God and humanity – not by sign but in reality. The priest is in a state of mediation between God and humanity by means of a sacrament, a sign. Yet we too can help the world through a spiritual mediation, a spiritual priesthood that draws its efficacy from the reality of our spiritual being.

The spiritual riches of Anglicanism, Roman Catholicism and Eastern Orthodoxy, especially the Christian mystical texts, had long nourished my soul like a secret watercourse, often finding expression through my writing and radio presentations. Yet even though I had cast myself in the guise of a searching itinerant, I think I had more than a hunch that, however obscure the prospect, there would come a time when I would have to cross the rubicon and pitch my tent in a camp. The litmus test was whether or not I had the tenacity to forego independence in my ambiguous quest for that not-so-distant land. But I completely identified with Brother Roger of Taizé when he said that he could reconcile the faith of his origins with the mystery of the Catholic Church without breaking fellowship with anyone.

A WEDDING AND FOUR FUNERALS

A turning point on the spiritual road began a couple of years later at a small twelfth-century church in West London where I had been invited to read the Gospel at the marriage blessing of close friends from the religious broadcasting world. As I walked towards the chancel and turned towards the congregation, I found myself staring at a gallery of journalistic faces, a number of whom were well known. Many had worked with me at some time or another but this was probably the first time they had witnessed me bowing to the altar and proclaiming the Word of God, something I had done for most of my life but not in front of my colleagues. As I looked down at the lectern and up again at the congregation, I felt the tension and exhilaration of a turning point, as though I were being cast into a completely new role. The journalistic past was yielding to a new way of spiritual being I could hardly believe or fathom.

I had planned to return home after the ceremony. But following the reception and a social gathering in Ealing, a few of us ended

WATERSHED

up at Ronnie Scott's jazz club in Soho (once nominated in a Radio 4 poll as a contender for Britain's most popular spiritual place: a reminder of that ushered us in). By then it was too late for the last rail connection so, without an overnight bag, I hastily purchased a few essentials and checked into a hotel in Piccadilly. The next morning, awake early and spared a hangover, there was only one matter on my mind – I needed a retreat. Immediately. With an impulsiveness, fed by spiritual zeal, I booked a seat on Eurostar and a few hours later was walking the streets of Paris. There has always been a sort of contemplative restlessness about me so spiritual oases require more movement than confinement. I decided to make use of the time travelling by train across northern France. I was in no hurry. There was time for daydreaming through the carriage windows. I concluded that I needed to wean myself away from journalism. But not too abruptly. The old existence had to die naturally before a new life could be born.

It was at lunchtime one early October morning, after attending a Mass in the abbey chapel at Mont Saint-Michel, in the ever-changing light of the rocky tidal island on the Normandy–Brittany border, that the distant possibility of becoming an ordained priest progressively came into focus – like the formation of a print in a developing tray.

On my return home, instead of feverishly monitoring bulletins at the sound of the alarm, I resolved to live more monastically, keeping my journalistic work to a minimum and aligning myself with broadcasting strands more akin to my new sense of calling. Slowly my life entered a less frenetic rhythm. I felt more relaxed and integrated. I found myself at home in a range of pastoral situations, while the privilege of being asked to take the funeral services of four friends in the local crematorium chapel at different times of the year appeared to authenticate the vocation further. Walking in a white monastic alb in front of the coffin seemed as natural to me as

ABANDONMENT AND TRUST

covering a story. Then, after researching a book about the priestly ministries of Thomas Merton, Henri Nouwen, Anthony de Mello and John O'Donohue, *Spiritual Masters for All Seasons*, I began to ask myself why I was always writing about priests instead of becoming one.[21] I conjectured that I didn't have too much by way of defence. But I needed the church to ratify the calling.

A crucial factor holding me back, I suppose, had been the one propelling me forward: a sense of vulnerability. The Archbishop of Canterbury, Dr Rowan Williams, has written that the ordained minister 'shares in the public perception the same important unclarity that hangs around the Church of England's identity: the same vulnerability to dismissive or derisive perception on the one hand, the same vulnerability to endless and shapeless demands on the other'.[22] He sees the *raison d'être* of ordained ministry as speaking of the church's transcendent origin and horizon, witnessing to the nature of the space that God clears, an undefended territory created by God's displacement of divine power.

In a further reflection on priesthood, Father James Hanvey SJ discusses the hiddenness and vulnerability of priestly life. 'He knows that he was not called for his strengths but for his weakness. He knows that those consoling words of Paul, that God's strength is perfected in his weakness, are not empty words.'[23]

It was this kenotic understanding of loving service to others through an emptying of self that also proved persuasive.

As the Irish philosopher-poet John O'Donohue has noted, a cleric is someone who attempts to be a priest from the outside in, adopting the uniform, behaviour and language of the institution. The clerical role subsumes the complexity, conflict and depth of individual interiority. It fails to offer a welcoming context for intimacy, doubt or sexuality. The true priest, on the other hand, lives from the inside out and is naturally drawn to the frontiers. But the edge is a precarious place. O'Donohue writes:

> Priesthood which embraces imagination will be deeply enriching and creative. It will have a natural hospitality to all areas and kinds of experience. It will not set safe frontiers and indulge in the criss-cross monologues of the like-minded. Such priesthood will risk conversation with the alienated, the post-religious and the indifferent.[24]

That was the kind of ministry I could relate to and I moved forward, though the demons still lingered from time to time. Imaginary scenarios of future confinement cast their self-doubting shadows. However, after interviewing one of the miners who had been trapped underground in Chile, I soon gained a sense of perspective. Then, as winter turned slowly into spring, my sense of vocation began to bud, any reluctance tempered by words of Henri Nouwen:

> As you see more clearly that your vocation is to be a witness to God's love in this world, and as you become more determined to live out that vocation, the attacks of the enemy will increase ... The more you sense God's call, the more you will discover in your own soul the cosmic battle between God and Satan. Do not be afraid. Keep deepening your conviction that God's love for you is enough, that you are in safe hands, and that you are being guided every step of the way. Don't be surprised by the demonic attacks. They will increase, but as you face them without fear, you will discover that they are powerless.[25]

ENDINGS AND BEGINNINGS

Words of the Benedictine nun Maria Boulding gave credence to what seemed to be happening to me:

> There may seem to be good reasons for not going (whether the 'going' that is being asked includes some outward step or not):

ABANDONMENT AND TRUST

there is work we can do for the Lord without that; indeed, to go may spell the end of our usefulness. At the same time we know that this one thing is being asked and we cannot evade it, at any rate not for long, and that anything else we may be doing will lose its meaning if we refuse that call.[26]

I thought back to the day I had met the late Dame Maria, a biblical scholar of international repute, when her community at Stanbrook Abbey in Worcestershire, England, announced they were selling up and moving to an eco-friendly monastery in Yorkshire. I recalled the icy December morning when I had been on another train heading to the Malverns to enquire how the sisters were to spend (what they then thought would be) their last Christmas. There, in the chapel, sat Dame Maria who, at the time, had been at member of the community for over 58 years.

Maria Boulding realised she was destined to become a nun when she was about 16. But it had not been a spectacular intervention. She wasn't even praying at the time, merely looking out of a window. It was as though the truth had been in her mind for a long while but she had only just turned to look directly at it – to recognise consciously that it was there. She likened the experience to being in a room with another person when your eyes are not on them; then, at some moment, you turn and look.

Dame Maria had arrived at Stanbrook one autumn day in 1947 but told me that she still found it difficult to articulate precisely why she had turned up. For most monks and nuns, she said, the reason you come is not the same as the reason you stay. 'People come for all sorts of strange reasons really, attracted by something or other, but you soon find out that, whatever that something-or-other was, it is not going to see you through a lifetime. So you have to rethink your motives a good deal.

'I suppose one can say it's a response to the love of God that one has known in one's life somehow. God makes himself known in

WATERSHED

every person's life, *every* person somehow or other. Some of us follow that love that calls in this monastic way. It's only one way among a myriad of others of living out the response to God in Christ, living out our baptism. This is just one way. But it's a way that has been classic in Christianity from the beginning and still does call many men and women today.'

Contemplation was plodding on in faith, in darkness, in the desert for much or even most of the time, an all too familiar pattern for monastics. The desert was a definite part of the chosen people's life. It had always existed in the church as Jesus himself chose to go into the desert for a key period in his life. So struggle was integral to the spiritual life in general, she explained, let alone the discernment of a call. Searching and finding were all of a piece.

So, said Dame Maria, vocation was a lifelong search but at the same time a person could not be seeking unless they had, in some way, already found. 'God is infinitely beyond us, *infinitely* beyond us,' she went on. 'We'll never come to the end of God or think we've got him sorted out and taped. It's not like that. Even in heaven, presumably, when we see him face to face, I suppose we go on seeking. I don't know. St Augustine ventures to say he thinks possibly we do, so I'm in good company. But you seek and you find, and you find and you seek. And you never come to the end of God.'

TESTING THE CALL

The railway station at Ely, on the main line from King's Cross to King's Lynn, lies in the 'Holy Land of the English' known as the Fens. Adorned with flowering plants and shrubs, it once won an award as best cycle-rail station, one of those incidental details that bizarrely grabs your attention as you try to take your mind off the purpose for which you have arrived – a Bishops' Advisory Panel.

It is also the kind of irrelevance that might emerge in the warm-up conversations over coffee with the selectors when, with your future

ABANDONMENT AND TRUST

in their hands, you are unable to think of anything remotely sensible to say. For weeks they have been studying your sponsoring papers, absorbing all the intimate details about your pilgrimage of faith. Now they come face to face with the person the documents purport to portray. The test is whether or not you will match up to what you have said about yourself and what others have said about you.

The conference (timed with precision 'from Monday at 5 pm to Wednesday at 3.45 pm') is chaired by a Panel secretary. The process is marked throughout by professionalism and warmth. As I watch it unfold, it is difficult to imagine a more impressive side of the Church of England, a meticulous procedure undergirded with prayer and liturgy.

Searching interviews and taxing pastoral exercises, along with prepared presentations and team work, are assessed against nine criteria for selection. The sixteen candidates are divided into two groups. Each has its own vocational, pastoral and educational advisers who, with forms, pens and stopwatches, observe, note and time. But, unlike the driving test, this is not about passing or failing: the road to ordination should never inculcate a sense of superiority in anyone. On the contrary, it obliges you to divest yourself so you can prepare for a ministry of service to others through a life open to Christ.

... As I wait at home for the outcome, it seems sensible not to cower before the verdict as though it were The Last Judgment. But the thoroughness and empathy which has accompanied the process at every stage, from diocesan discernment to national testing, convinces me that, whatever the result, my sense of vocation to the priesthood has been taken seriously (and explored fairly) by the church. Furthermore, I have learned much about myself – and my self in relationship with others – that might not have been so evident without such scrupulous and respectful inquiry. In itself, the experience of testing the call has been a process of growth and transformation, a turning point on the spiritual freeway.

WATERSHED

CROSSING THE RUBICON

Four months later, with my 'recommendation for training' documents safely packed, I load the car and head off to Ripon College, Cuddesdon, in the heart of the Oxfordshire countryside. It is shortly before Michaelmas and, indeed, the demons are hovering: I soon realize that seminaries can be places where cosmic hostilities of the soul are played out. 'Holy Michael, the Archangel, defend us in the day of battle.'

There are several inner confrontations in the weeks ahead as I gradually adjust to a way of life where, in the intensity of growing together, one's emotions and struggles are laid bare. It proves a difficult transition for me at first as I yearn for my former securities. I understand what Mother Dolores Hart meant when she told me, 'You have to find in your own heart the meaning of what you have done.'

But slowly, almost imperceptibly, I discern that something profound is, in fact, happening and I come to realise that, through the liturgy, the lectures, the croquet and the constant fellowship, I am undergoing a spiritual transformation in order to enter a new life. It is undoubtedly a death and resurrection experience, and one also shared by those I am training with. Above all, it is this sense of being part of a community of love which helps me through the watershed and engages me in a world of new friendships which I know will sustain me in the years ahead. Here I am conscious of being reshaped among people for whom I have immense respect and deep affection.

As I write, my ordination to holy orders is on the horizon and already I feel the pain of having to leave behind a world which has become so much part of me. But I know also that losses can be transfigured. The journey towards priesthood involves letting go and being caught. That is what all watersheds are about.

POSTLUDE

As we have discovered, a watershed is an experience that marks or changes us. It can appear gradually on the horizon or it can come upon us unexpectedly. Moreover, it is not unusual to find ourselves moving through several watersheds in the course of one life.

A pastoral counsellor and writer in Seattle, Dr Thomas Hart, sees watershed experiences as deeply challenging events. They are often characterised by one way of life coming to an end before another has been revealed. There is a crisis of meaning when we feel out of control and afraid. Hart says human growth happens more or less constantly, but again, imperceptibly, as we make our responses. Such times are especially significant for who we will become and the kind of self we will create:

> That is because these critical junctures challenge us much more deeply. There is new learning, there is a painful stretching of our capacities, and there are crucial choices to make.
>
> Growth, unfortunately, is not guaranteed. It comes at a price. When we come to one of these turning points, we can get stuck and stay stuck, never moving on to life's next stage. We can even regress to an earlier level of development. Or we can summon up our courage and pass over into the new. It is something like the Hebrew people in the desert, caught between two lands.[27]

How we cope and how open we are to growth depends on many factors but what seems clear from the stories in this book and my own experience is that while a major turning point may result in loss and suffering, it can also lead to interior depth and spiritual renewal. There may be an ending but there will also be a beginning.

As I look back on these encounters which took place over a decade or more, I sense that faith is not something we need to strive for as such – but to discover at the very heart of our choosing, seeking, doubting and struggling.

When we find ourselves in crisis, faith is the act of carrying on hopefully, trusting that, somehow, we will become stronger people through our trials and tragedies, our callings to new life and undiscovered realities.

The pilgrimage of faith is a process of trust and discernment. It is not about solving all the problems life presents but about learning to negotiate those turning points with care and creativity – as well as exchanging our personal stories of human and spiritual experience with those we meet on the road.

All our lives we are creatures of becoming, always incomplete, always growing (or regressing), always pilgrims and discoverers. (Maria Boulding)

NOTES

1. N. Wilkie Au, *The Enduring Heart: Spirituality for the Long Haul*, Paulist Press, 2000, p. 83.
2. The interview was originally broadcast on *Heart and Soul*, BBC World Service, Autumn 2006.
3. Maggie Ross, *Pillars of Flame*, SCM Press, 1988, pp. 16–17. The book was republished by Seabury in 2007.
4. Maggie Ross, *Writing the Icon of the Heart: In Silence Beholding*, Bible Reading Fellowship, 2011.
5. H. A. Williams, *Becoming Who I Am*, Darton Longman and Todd, 1977, p. 19.
6. James Martin SJ, *Becoming Who You Are*, HiddenSpring, 2006, p. 17.
7. Coleman Barks with John Moyne (trans.), *The Essential Rumi*, Castle Books, 1997, p. 34.
8. William H. Shannon (ed.), *The Hidden Ground of Love: The Letters of Thomas Merton on Religious Experience and Social Concerns*, Collins, 1985, p. 387.
9. Gerald G. May MD, *Addiction and Grace: Love and Spirituality in the Healing of Addictions*, HarperSanFrancisco, 1988, p. 4.
10. André Louf, *Tuning in to Grace: The Quest for God*, Cistercian Publications, 1992.
11. Henri J. M. Nouwen, *The Inner Voice of Love: A Journey through Anguish to Freedom*, Doubleday, 1996, p. 110.
12. Bernard Miles, 'Why Must the Show Go On?' in Dick Richards (comp.), *The Curtain Rises: An Anthology of the International Theatre*, Leslie Frewin Publishers, 1966, p. 44.

13 Grace Sheppard, *An Aspect of Fear: A Journey from Anxiety to Peace*, Darton, Longman and Todd, 2010.

14 Mark Oakley, *The Collage of God*, Darton Longman and Todd, 2001.

15 Jean-Pierre de Caussade, *Abandonment to Divine Providence*, Image, Doubleday, 1975, p. 83.

16 Ibid., pp. 81–2.

17 Ibid., p. 60.

18 St John Chrysostom, *Six Books on the Priesthood*, St Vladimir's Seminary Press, 1984, pp. 41–2.

19 Michael Ford, *Song of the Nightingale: A Modern Spiritual Canticle*, Paulist Press, 2005.

20 Jean-Marie Howe OCSO, *Spiritual Journey: The Monastic Way*, St Bede's Publications, 1989.

21 Michael Ford, *Spiritual Masters for All Season*, HiddenSpring, 2010.

22 Samuel Wells and Sarah Coakley (eds), *Praying for England: Priestly Presence in Contemporary Culture*, Continuum 2008, p. 179.

23 Fr John Hanvey SJ, 'The Hiddenness of Priestly Life', in Daniel P. Cronin (ed.), *Priesthood: A Life Open to Christ*, St Paul's Publishing, 2009, p. 72.

24 John O'Donohue, 'Minding the Threshold: Towards a Theory of Priesthood in Difficult Times', *The Furrow*, vol. 49, no. 6, June 1998, p. 328.

25 Nouwen, *The Inner Voice of Love*, p. 93.

26 Maria Boulding, *The Coming of God*, The Printery House, Conception Abbey, Missouri, 2000, pp. 112–13.

27 Thomas Hart, *Coming Down the Mountain: How to Turn your Retreat into Everyday Living*, Paulist Press, 1988, pp. 95–6.

ACKNOWLEDGEMENTS

I am, of course, indebted to all those I encountered 'on the spiritual road' who entrusted their stories so graciously. It seemed appropriate, therefore, to dedicate this book to Kristine Pommert and David Coomes with whom I have worked on many stories at the BBC. Their close friendship and spiritual insights are much valued; indeed it was their wedding (as recounted in chapter nine) which inaugurated my own vocational watershed. I am particularly grateful to my mother, Margaret, and brother, Nigel, who have been unfailingly generous in many ways as the journey has unfolded.

I should also like to acknowledge the support of the diocese of Bath and Wells especially that of Bishop Peter Price, Bishop Peter Maurice and Prebendary Dr Catherine Wright, director of ordinands, as well as the encouragement of Michael Bardouleau, Sally Buddle, Ken and Phyllis Burge, Sheila Cook, Geoff Driver, Sebastian Gillies, Ainsley Griffiths, Stuart Halstead, Caroline Hewitt, Eva Heymann, Peter and Jane Huxham, Irene Jones, Clair Jaquiss, Tony Lee, Giles Legood, Paul Lewis, Rodney Middleton, Robin Pettitt, Mark Oakley, Tim Pike, Anne Reynolds, Peter Scott, Stephen Shipley, Val Simpson, David Stead, Justine Sturman and David Torevell, along with members of St Andrew's and St John's, Taunton; St Pancras, West Bagborough; St James the Great, Haydock; All Saints' Catholic Church, Golborne; and St Peter's Catholic Church, Big Pine Key, Florida.

My immense gratitude to the Rev Canon Professor Martyn Percy (principal), the Rev Raymond Tomkinson (chaplain) and all staff on 'God's holy hill' for their excellent teaching and guidance. As I moved from the studio to the seminary, former BBC colleague

WATERSHED

Christopher Landau, now himself an ordinand here, helped me bridge those worlds with such generosity of heart.

My fellow seminarians have all displayed love, friendship and a spirit of attentive prayerfulness. Special thanks to Alastair Blaine, Lee Taylor and Richard Whaite for their engaging conversations, good humour, and spiritual accompaniment; to my 'BAP brother' John Roles for his wisdom and mirth; to David Cowie for his thoughtful kindness; and to Sam Cross, Geoff Dumbreck, Christopher Johnson, Myles Owen, Laurence Powell, Mark Woodrow and Josh Young for their constant fellowship. I'm grateful to many other residential students who have shared the pilgrimage with me, among them: Nick Adley and Pip, Tom Albinson, Simon Archer, Matthew Barrett, Lesley Bilinda, Felicity Blair, Tom Birch, Tom Carson, Matt Cottrell, Andrew Down, Yvonne Greener, Doug and Zoe Heming, Tina Kelsey, Suzanne Leighton, Andrew Lightbown, Steve Marsh, Michelle Martin, Alison Mathew, Annie McCabe, James McDonald, Sheena McMain, Simon McMurtary, Sam Moores, Gill Nobes, John Overton, Richard Phillips, Christopher Pickles Andy Trenier and Diana Young.

As always, it has been a joy to work again with Virginia Hearn, my creative editor at DLT. Thanks also to Brendan Walsh, Helen Porter, Will Parkes and all the production team in London.